Rejoice in Your Work

A 44-Day Devotional for Finding
Contentment in God's Plan
for Your Work

Cindy Schwerdtfeger

Dedication

*To the LORD God, Jesus Christ, and the Holy Spirit
— You are the One who called me out from the path that
I was walking on and rescued me. You are the reason
why this book came to being and was completed.
Thank you, Lord!*

Table of Contents

Introduction

Everyone also to whom God has given wealth and possessions and power to enjoy them, and to accept his lot and rejoice in his toil --- this is the gift of God. For he will not much remember the days of his life because God keeps him occupied with joy in his heart. Ecclesiastes 5:19-20

Work satisfaction. I have longed for satisfaction in my life and my work for as long as I can remember.

As a young girl, I couldn't wait to grow up, finish high school, and grow up to achieve great things as an adult. I wanted to find the man of my dreams and have the perfect children. And I wanted the job that would bring me great satisfaction in life and the accolades that went with it.

I graduated from high school and college, found the man of my dreams, and had two *almost* perfect Jesus-loving children. They both have made me a proud momma for all their accomplishments, and I love being Oma to our grandchildren.

But none of the jobs that I have done satisfied my longing for contentment, peace, acceptance, and the accolades of a job well done.

God is the only one that I have found who provides all this and more. After a sudden change in my employment, I changed from determining my path was better than what God had for me to following His plan for my life and trust Him with the outcome. When I surrendered control of my life back to Him and humbly submitted to His Will, I found that His plan is the way to that life of peace and the satisfaction or joy within my heart to rejoice in my work.

I pray that as you read this devotional and study God's Word you will find contentment in God's plan for your work. And that will cause you to rejoice in your work!

Many humble and heartfelt blessings to you~
Cindy Schwerdtfeger

How to Use this Devotional

If this is your first devotional reading ever, congratulations on your purchase! I am humbled and honored that you chose this book.

Here are some tips on how to use this book.

1) Start with a Prayer. Ask God to infuse you with the Holy Spirit as you read His Word, to give you the insight into what He wants you to learn.
2) Read the scripture at the top of the devotional and any look up the scripture passage(s) listed in the Read heading at the bottom of the devotional. Be sure to read the context of the verses.
3) Then read through the devotional for the day.
4) Answer the questions in the action step.
5) Pray the suggested prayer or whatever comes to your mind.

These steps are outlined in more detail on page 178. This is the READ study method that I designed for us to learn how to dig deeper into God's Word.

If you don't know how you can have Peace with God, see page 176. This is the basis of your relationship with God, Jesus, and the Holy Spirit. This will help you understand why it is important to have a personal relationship with God.

If you have read devotionals before and you have the steps above down, feel free to dig into the first day and examine God's Word.

May God bless you in the reading and studying of His Word!

Cindy

Section One:

Surrendering Control to God

DAY ONE

Exquisite Delight

"Delight yourself in the Lord and
He will give you the desires of your heart."
Psalm 37:4

My boss spoke the job-ending words that I dreaded. Anger built up within me as I listened to his eloquent explanation that my desire for promotion within the department was not going to be a possibility.

I had been given a choice of taking a position within another Information Services (I.S.) department or my severance and leave. The other job was a step up, but it wasn't the position I desired and worked for in my department.

Maybe you've experienced something similar where your career came to a crashing halt or the path you have chosen for a dream job is hitting a dead end. And now you are questioning your desires for your work.

As I began to realize that my desires might not match God's desires, one of my favorite verses came to mind:

> *"Delight yourself in the Lord, and He will give you the desires of your heart." (Psalm 37:4 ESV)*

If I was delighting in Him, wasn't He going to give me the desires of my heart?

The Hebrew word for delight means to be happy about or take exquisite delight in. Webster's Dictionary defines exquisite, in this context, as "having uncommon appeal."

My field in technology was appealing to me. But, like any job, there was a downside. Some of the work was frustrating. I was also stressed, and my health was showing it.

Even with the stress, however, I took pleasure in what I did and how I could get ahead. I was blind to the fact that I was not genuinely delighting in the Lord. I was promoting my selfish desires instead of God. No wonder my desires did not align with His!

Maybe you, too, need to examine yourself to see if you are delighting in the Lord. What is the motive behind your desires? Is it to promote yourself or to promote God?

You are likely wondering, as I did, how do I understand what it means to delight in Him?

My first giant step was the hardest. I asked God to humble me, and I surrendered my desires to Him. With my desire for promotion removed, I was ready to delight in Him and His plan for me.

I was taking exquisite delight in Him by seeking His counsel in all areas. Once my focus was on delighting Him, then my desires came into alignment with His desires.

Once we empty ourselves of our selfish desires and listen for God's desires for us, we become more in tune with who He is and what He desires for us. His desires become our desires.

Do you take exquisite delight in the Lord? Are your desires in alignment with His desires?

God has a better plan for your desires when you surrender control to Him and take exquisite delight in Him.

Key: Our desires may not match the desires God has for us. God desires us to delight in Him.

Read: Psalm 37:4; Hebrews 12:11

Action: What desires do you need to give to God so you can focus on Him?

Prayer Moment: Lord, I give You this desire that is serving me instead of You. Help me to focus on You, Lord. I desire to do Your will. Lead me to the desires and the plan You have for me. Amen.

DAY TWO

Are You a Control Freak?

"'For my thoughts are not your thoughts, neither are your ways my ways,' declares the Lord. 'For as the heavens are higher than the earth, so are my ways higher than your ways and my thoughts than your thoughts.'" Isaiah 55:8-9 ESV

Genuine Control Freak.

If that were a branding iron, it would be marked on my hind quarter. Thankfully, I am not a cow!

Remember school group projects? I'd take control if no one jumped in, even after waiting only a few milliseconds. The silence and inaction would kill me.

I have done the same with work. With every breakout discussion group, I jumped in to take charge. Or when the boss requested volunteers and the room went silent, I'd be the one to volunteer.

If God's answer to my prayer is absent or even tardy, I dive in without Him.

Yikes! Are you going alone without God like me? Do you jump in to take control when God is silent?

In Isaiah 55:8-9, God says,

> *"'For my thoughts are not your thoughts, neither are your ways my ways,' declares the Lord. 'For as the heavens are higher than the earth, so are my ways higher than your ways and my thoughts than your thoughts.'"*

The Hebrew word for ways is *derek*, which means a course of life or mode of action. This word can be a physical path or a metaphor for a pattern or pathway in life.

We don't understand His ways or thoughts. Selfish desires, impatience, and pride all take center stage when we want to be in control. And God is placed on a shelf.

God has the bigger picture of our lives, and we need to relinquish control to Him. If tragedy has struck, unanswered prayers abound, or you feel stuck, surrendering the situation is the answer.

Even when it seems like your world is falling apart, He knows what's going on. He is with you.

I felt that way when I was diagnosed with fibromyalgia. I was unsure why this was happening, but I had to give God control. He knew the bigger plan and would care for me in this situation.

Thankfully, two years later, another physician reversed that diagnosis and referred me to my general practice doctor. My provider and I began the journey of sourcing out the pain. God knew what I needed. Over time, I have found simple solutions in vitamins, diet, and stress management.

Remember that God's ways and thoughts are higher than ours. We need to let our control freakiness go and let Him be in control. He is much better at it than we are.

Key: Remember that God's ways and thoughts are higher than ours. He is in control and knows what is best for us.

Read: Isaiah 55:8-9; Psalm 139:17

Action Step:
What area of your work (or life) do you need to allow God to take control? Give that area to God now and ask Him to be in control of it.

Prayer Moment:
Lord, help me to give You control. You need to be in control and not me. Your ways are higher than mine and the best for me. Help me to accept that and move on. Amen.

DAY THREE

Surrender and Sacrifice

"'And I will make of you a great nation, and I will bless you and make your name great, so that you will be a blessing.'" Genesis 12:2

We all have hopes, dreams, and desires that we want to happen. However, they may become glorified in our minds, and we neglect to think of the barriers and hurdles needed to get there.

Most of the time we discover that sacrifice is required so that the bright lights on the dream don't go dim. Sometimes we must sacrifice the dream itself.

Have you made a sacrifice to obtain your dream? What if God called you to sacrifice what was most precious to you?

Abraham was promised to be a father and many nations would be blessed through him (Genesis 12:2-3). Through God's miraculous power, He opened

Sarah's dried-up womb, at 90 years old, to have a baby! Abraham and Sarah experienced the blessings of having a child from a promise. It was a miracle that Isaac had been born to parents at their age. But their trust in God for the miraculous wasn't over yet.

When Isaac was twelve years old, God asked Abraham to sacrifice his son. God didn't choose his illegitimate son that he had with Hagar, Sarah's handmaid. God chose the one who would make him the promised father of many nations. We can imagine the confusion Abraham and Sarah must have felt. How would God's promise come true? And why would God ask this of them? It seemed too much. The sacrifice wasn't the most obvious, but it was the most precious.

The ending of the story is better than you think. God provided the sacrifice at the right moment. When Abraham raised his knife to slaughter his son, a ram suddenly appeared and was caught in the thicket nearby. His son was spared. God honored Abraham's willingness to sacrifice what was most precious to him.

My job had become an idol that I was putting before God. God wasn't answering my prayers about what I should do next with my work life, so I took control. My work ambition became front and center while God took a near second.

I didn't need to consult God for every decision at work. But I should have consulted him on the big things, like seeking a promotion or getting a second master's degree.

Upon finishing my degree, I pressed on harder towards the promotion and power I desired. Becoming a manager in a specialized field had become like a precious child to me that was hard to let go of.

Unlike Abraham's story, my "job child" was sacrificed. Yet God provided for me. His provision came as a job within the same company but under a God-honoring boss who loves the Lord.

That submission to God has released stress, improved my health, and given me more peace because I am doing God's plan for me. The blessings I have received allow me to serve God and bless others in ways that I have not done before.

These blessings come when we surrender to God and sacrifice the most precious dreams that we need to leave at His feet.

Key: You need to be willing to surrender and sacrifice things you hold close so you can receive God's blessing.

Read: Genesis 12:2-3; Romans 12:1

Action: What in your life do you need to surrender sacrificially to God? Make your "sacrifice" to God and ask for help to leave it at His feet.

Prayer Moment: Lord, I leave this precious sacrifice at Your feet. Help me to leave it with You and not take it back. I surrender to the plan You have for me to do, and I humbly honor You. Amen.

DAY FOUR

Idol Runner

"'You will know the truth and the truth will set you free.'" John 8:32

ou shall know the truth and the truth

shall set you free."

That verse was on the wall of my junior high when I walked into the building. It caught my attention, so I knew that when I got home, I wanted to find that Scripture reference.

Arriving home that night, I poured through the Bible looking for the words. The internet didn't exist so I couldn't ask Alexa, Siri, or Google to find the answer for me. I found the verse was in John 8:32.

The truth in these words comes from abiding or living continually in accordance with His Words. When we live abundantly in His truth, we are free. Conversely, if we aren't living in God's truth, we live in slavery to some other idol.

Idols today come in different forms. Celebrities, sports figures, and even your boss can be people we idolize. Things we do like hobbies, working out, or our jobs can be an idol.

My desire to be promoted and get ahead was at the forefront of my mind. I woke up thinking about work. I worked many hours each day. And if there was a deadline, I was working late at night at home. I'd go to bed thinking about work and even dream about work. My job was all- encompassing and had become an idol in my life.

Do you have an idol in your life that has become all-consuming like mine was? Is it taking first place in your life instead of God?

The Israelites in the Old Testament were given instructions by God about idols. When they moved into the Promised Land, they were to tear down the altars of the foreign gods (Exodus 34:13). No one or nothing should take the place of God. Not only is God jealous of who or what you call your god, but His name is also called Jealous (Exodus 34:14).

Without tearing down the idols, the Israelites would be tempted to follow the ways of the people living in the land. The idols had to come down to remain true to serving God and God alone. They needed to run far from the idols and run to God.

Similarly, In the New Testament, we read that the Holy Spirit gives us freedom:

"Now the Lord is the Spirit, and where the Spirit of the Lord is, there is freedom." (2 Corinthians 3:17)

When a person accepts Christ into their life, they receive the Holy Spirit. The Spirit guides, corrects, encourages, and protects. He has a big job! Yet when we yield to the truth of God's Word, we have freedom. That freedom is from the burden of the law and the ritual sacrifices of the Old Testament that were once needed to be given to atone for sin. Jesus was our ultimate sacrifice so the practice of giving animal sacrifices is no longer needed.

Are you finding yourself in bondage to an idol that you have created or have habitually given more of your life to?

People or things, like a job, don't guide us to God's truth in our lives. Nor do they lead us to the freedom we find in Him. When we run from these idols and into God's loving arms, we grow in His truth and obtain true freedom.

Key: Running from idols to God's loving arms will lead you to His truth and freedom.

Read: John 8:32; Exodus 34:13-14; 2 Corinthians 3:17

Action: What idols do you need to tear down and run into God's arms?

Prayer Moment: Lord, I am throwing this idol away and running into Your loving arms. Thank you for the truth that is in Your Word and the freedom that I find in You. Amen.

DAY FIVE

Restraining Your Words

"The heart of the righteous ponders how to answer, but the mouth of the wicked pours out evil things." Proverbs 15:28

The email announcement regarding the department restructures whooshed from my former boss's mailbox to all the recipients.

It was official. I was no longer the manager of the department and was now in a different reporting structure.

New emails flooded my inbox with well wishes, concern, and even congratulations on the promotion. However, the unexpected change caused a few co-workers concern, and they questioned what had happened. They asked if we could meet for coffee or lunch. I wholeheartedly accepted their invitations.

After the meeting with my boss and HR a week earlier, anger had boiled through my veins. I prayed daily for God to take these thoughts captive (2 Corinthians 10:5) and replace them with trust for His plan for me.

But it was hard. What were others thinking of me? Feelings of failure and unworthiness for what I had worked hard on were nagging me. How could I go to these meetings and explain what happened to me yet be respectful with my words?

Have you had that happen before? Something that makes you so mad or hurt you want to let all the words in your head spill out of your mouth. And then you regret it later. I have done that many times.

Yet, I had to let God take those thoughts captive. There were reasons He wanted me to stay put and not get a position in another company. If I let these evil thoughts erupt from my unrighteous anger and spew forth from my mouth about my former boss, they could get back to him and then I might be escorted out the company door.

I needed to glorify God by thinking about how to answer their questions respectfully. These words from Proverbs were at the forethought of my mind:

> *"The heart of the righteous ponders how to answer, but the mouth of the wicked pours out evil things." (Proverbs 15:28)*

Before the casual meetings, I prayed that I would be respectful of my former boss and bring honor to God with my words.

And so, I did as I had hoped. I explained how the meeting transpired and was honest about how I had walked out of the meeting in anger. Yet God was faithful in showing me He was in control and wanted me to pursue writing, while staying at the company. I shared how He had confirmed this by the words of others and His Word. I had honored God, and my thoughts of anger had not taken over.

Have you failed in retelling stories like me and let unholy words spill over about the people who hurt you? What about in other situations? Maybe when you're frustrated with your loved ones or kids? Or when you feel hurt by a friend?

Many times, I have spewed unrighteous words in anger. But this time I was able to do the right thing by focusing on God's Word and praying before each meeting with my co-workers.

The words we say and how we say them are significant.

No matter how many email announcements go out about us, or impolite things are said about us on social media, restraining our words reflects the righteous and holy life that God has called us to live.

Key: There is value in restraining our words. Restraining our words is the righteous and holy living that God has called us to.

Read: Proverbs 15:28; 2 Corinthians 10:5

Action: What is one thing you can do today to restrain your words?

Prayer Moment: Lord, forgive me for the words that I have said without thinking. Guide me to stop, pray, and restrain my words before I say them. I know that by doing this I will live the righteous and holy life You desire of me. Amen.

DAY SIX

Spirit-Mindedness

"For to set the mind on the flesh is death, but to set the mind on the Spirit is life and peace."
Romans 8:6

Peace. My favorite word in the Bible.

I have desired peace for years.

One summer my brother and I stayed with my grandparents while my parents went on a trip. My grandma had a cross-stitched picture of praying hands and the word peace above it.

We did a craft that week to take a picture and imprint it onto a hard plastic dinner plate. The picture on the wall of peace was the one I chose.

So why peace? At a young age, I aspired to do my best in everything I tried. Curiosity and a desire to learn new things had always been a part of my life. Yet my heart was unsettled.

God puts in us a desire to be filled and a longing for satisfaction. But striving after the things of the world fills us up with things that aren't meaningful. Instead, it causes stress. Stress leads to worry and a lack of peace.

Have you longed to be filled and satisfied? What have you tried to find satisfaction in? Maybe you've tried to fill yourself up with money, food, exercise, or relationships. Have you found those things satisfying?

Jesus knew about our desires and wanting to be filled. He knew that we would need peace. Before He left this world, He told the disciples that He would give them peace.

> *"'Peace I leave with you; my peace I give to you. Not as the world gives do I give to you. Let not your hearts be troubled, neither let them be afraid.'" (John 14:27)*

Jesus gave them the peace that was from Him. His peace. Not a peace that is found in this world. Peace isn't found in learning, getting to the top of the corporate ladder, having more money than what you need, or a perfectly toned body.

Peace comes from a relationship with Jesus himself. Once we accept Him, then we receive the Spirit. That Spirit dwells within us and it is life-giving.

That is why Paul said,

> *"For to set the mind on the flesh is death, but to set the mind on the Spirit is life and peace."* *(Romans 8:6)*

The mind is what controls our thoughts and purposes for what is in our hearts. When we focus our mind on things of this earth or the desires of our body it leads us down a destructive path. But when our minds dwell on the Holy Spirit we have that peace and the fulfilled life we seek.

The peace that I longed for was in my heart when I asked Jesus to come into my life before I stayed with my grandparents that summer. But I had spent years striving for things of the world that were bringing me closer to death instead of peace.

Many years later after that summer, my grandparents moved from their home to a senior living complex. That move meant downsizing a lifetime of possessions and I inherited the cross-stitched picture of the praying hands with peace at the top.

The Bible word that means so much to me is on prominent display in our house. It is a reminder that peace comes from God and is within us, not from the world and the things that we desire.

All I need to do is breathe in the Spirit to remind me of the peace I have within me every day.

Key: Having a mind controlled by the Spirit equals peace.

Read: Romans 8:6; John 10:10; John 14:27

Action: Make it a point today to memorize Romans 8:6. Exhale the mind of the flesh. Breath in deeply and inhale the Spirit of life and peace.

Prayer Moment: Lord, help me to breathe in your Spirit and exhale the desires of the world. Thank you for the peace and the full life that I can have in You. Amen.

DAY SEVEN

Release Your Treasures

"And he said to them, 'Take care, and be on your guard against all covetousness, for one's life does not consist in the abundance of his possessions.'" Luke 12:15

y job certification had become a

treasure to me.

I had worked in Information Security for almost 20 years when my position was eliminated, and I was forced to decide. I chose to stay at my current company as God had made it clear that is what He wanted me to do.

While in the new department, I began to look for other positions in security. I spent several years honing my craft. With any certification, continuing education is needed to keep it current. Security had become a hot button due to regulations and the soaring increase of cybercriminals. And with the recent push to have people work from home due to social distancing measures, the attacks were on the rise on home networks.

However, I needed to complete eighty credits within six months, or the hard-earned certification would expire.

I began to question the value of hanging onto this certification. Maybe God didn't want me to keep seeking this? Should I let the certification go to pursue greater things for God?

Over the next couple of months, I had three different signs through others that I believe God was letting me know it was time for this treasured certification to go.

What is your treasure? Your loved ones, house, job, car, or a special gift you received can all be items that you treasure.

Some may be things that you have spent years obtaining, training for, putting money away in savings for, or waiting for it to come into your life.

However, any or all these precious treasures can become an idol and keep you from an intimate relationship with God.

Jesus said this,

> "'Take care, and be on your guard against all covetousness, for one's life does not consist in the abundance of his possessions.'" (Luke 12:15)

Jesus continued with a parable of a man who had a plentiful harvest. This man wanted to tear down his current barns and build bigger ones. And the man told himself he had so many treasures that he could relax and not work. But he didn't know that he would die that night and the things he prepared would be left behind (vs.16-20). Jesus concluded with,

> "'So is the one who lays up treasure for himself and is not rich toward God.'" Luke 12:21

If we covet all these things in life and don't prepare our hearts for the richness we have in God, we lose so much more. We lose the ability to be content in God and how He satisfies us in life. And if we don't reach out to Him and accept Jesus as our Savior, we lose out on the rich life with Him in eternity.

None of these things in life will satisfy us the way God and His Word will richly delight us the most (Isaiah 55:2).

Grasping and clinging onto treasures prevent us from being truly satisfied. Open your hands and release those treasures to Him.

That one small yet hard act will bring you more satisfaction in God than you ever thought possible.

Key: Releasing your treasures leads to being rich in God.

Read: Luke 12:15-21; Isaiah 55:2

Action: What treasures in your work or other areas of your life are you holding onto that you need to let go and richly delight in God?

Prayer Moment: Lord, I release my treasures to You. Forgive me for hanging on to them and thinking they will satisfy me. Thank you for the treasure that I find in You. Amen.

DAY EIGHT

Release Your

Distractions

"Seek the LORD and his strength;
seek his presence continually!"
1 Chronicles 16:11

Squirrel!

When this word is said most people understand that you are talking about a distraction.

And I am so easily distracted. I often wonder how I get anything done when I am thinking about multiple things at once.

I am preoccupied with social media notifications, multi-tasking, and wanting something to do to keep me busy. Sitting still and listening is hard for me.

One of my most common distractions happens when I am in the kitchen cooking and trying to multitask at the same time. Usually, this doesn't end well. I start some bacon and begin working on the dishes.

I store my dishes neatly in the cupboards and put the dirty ones into the dishwasher. But my breakfast goes up in smoke and is now darker than my black Labrador Retriever. Now it is trash bound. Time and money are wasted, and I must begin breakfast preparations all over again.

Can you identify with being distracted? Have you been so distracted during your day that you forget something or someone important to you?

King David had thought of a remedy to keep His mind from being distracted.

He built houses for his family in Jerusalem, and he prepared a tent for the ark of the covenant in the city as well. He gathered all of Israel to bring the ark to the place where David had prepared for it to be. After sacrifices of burnt offerings and peace offerings, David wanted the people to remember all that God had done for them—miracles, judgments on other nations, and battles won. To remember this, he wrote songs of thanksgiving to be sung of God's faithfulness to them.

A line in one of those songs is special to me:

> *"Seek the Lord and his strength; seek his presence continually." (1 Chronicles 16:11)*

But we, like the Israelites, get distracted by other things in our life that take our focus off what God has done for us. When we zone in on those other things, we are hurting ourselves and others around us. We need to remember that the Lord is near us, and we can rely on His strength to support us *continually*.

Even when breakfast becomes a "burnt offering," it can be a reminder of what God has done for me and how I need to seek Him continually. I need to put the distractions aside and focus on Him. When God is my focal point, life is so much easier. He infuses me with the strength I need to tackle anything that I may encounter in my day.

What distractions or squirrels are keeping you from relying on God and from frequently seeking to be in His presence?

Release your distractions and focus on Him. It will turn your heart to thankfulness, and you will be reminded of all the blessings that He has graciously given to you.

Key: Distractions can hurt us and keep us from enjoying uninterrupted interaction with the Lord.

Read: 1 Chronicles 16:1-36

Action: Put your distractions aside today and focus on God. Spend time with Him today and thank Him for all your blessings.

Prayer Moment: Lord, help me to release my distractions. I need to put You at the center and rely on Your strength. Thank you for all the blessings You have given me. Amen.

DAY NINE

Put Down Your Worry Weights

"Cast all your anxieties on him, because he cares for you." 1 Peter 5:7

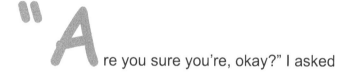

"**A**re you sure you're, okay?" I asked

my husband on the phone. "Do we need to come home?"

The kids and I had gone ahead to the Wednesday night children's program and youth group. My husband would be coming in his truck separate from us.

I dropped our son off to join the children's program, and our daughter joined me as I was getting things ready to start the youth group meeting.

But my heart was heavy. I was worried about Dave and his safety. I had been praying for him to make it to church safely through the rush hour traffic.

While I was in the youth room, our Pastor's wife yelled to me that I had a phone call. Dave had been driving through an intersection less than a mile from our home. A man had run the red light and Dave's truck had spun around in circles on the median taking out the road signs. He wasn't going to make it to church as his new truck had been totaled.

My prayer about Dave making it to church safely wasn't answered. But God had kept him safe, and he was at home! Praise the Lord!

Whenever Dave leaves the house, I worry that he will be in an accident, die, and then I won't be able to share life with him anymore.

Do you have those worries too? Can you relate? Do you worry when a loved one leaves the house, thinking maybe you won't see them again?

Peter said,

> *"Cast all your anxieties on him, because he cares for you." (1 Peter 5:7)*

God cares for us, and He knows what we need. We need to put our worries on Him. Even if the unimaginable happens, God has a plan, and He will take care of us.

Instead of worrying, I've learned to pray. Worries weigh me down. Praying gives me peace. And I need to praise God for what He has done for me.

In that accident, Dave said he felt like an angel was holding him safely in his truck as it spun around. God does care for us! And he will send his angels to guard us (Psalm 91:11-12).

King David experienced the same thing with worry. In Psalm 43, David asked God to defend him from injustice. He took refuge in God and wondered if God was rejecting him. He was feeling oppressed by his enemy. So, he asked God to let His light and truth lead him (vs 3).

David said,

> *"I will go to the altar of God, to God my exceeding joy, and I will praise you with the lyre, O God, my God." (Psalm 43:4)*

He knew that God's light and truth would lead him. He did not need to worry about his enemy. He needed to seek his source of joy, God himself, and spend time praising Him instead.

The next time you are riddled with worry, like I was about Dave being in an accident, let the worry weights go. In lieu of worry, spend time praying and praising God.

Give those worries to Him. Then praise God who is your exceeding joy for all that He has done for you.

Key: Worrying about things that may not happen steals your joy. Alternatively, spend time praising God who is the source of joy.

Read: 1 Peter 5:7; Psalm 43:3-4; Psalm 91:11-12

Action: What worries do you need to give to God so you can praise Him and receive His joy?

Prayer Moment: Lord, I give You, my worries. They are weighing me down, and I need You to lift them off my shoulders. I praise You for all You have done and will do for me! You are my exceeding joy! Amen.

DAY TEN

Release Your Past

"Now to him who is able to do far more abundantly than all that we ask or think, according to the power at work within us."
Ephesians 3:20

Have you experienced a change in your life that was totally devastating, a situation where you had to pick up the pieces and move on?

The Old Testament story of Ruth's experience was a change like that. Her husband, a foreigner to her country, had died. Since her father-in-law had also died, her mother-in-law, Naomi, wanted Ruth to forget her and stay behind as she moved back to Israel.

Ruth told Naomi that she couldn't follow through with that:

"'For where you go I will go, and where you lodge I will lodge. Your people shall be my people, and your God my God.'" (Ruth 1:16)

Ruth belonged to God and the people that she had married into. She was giving up her past and recent tragedy to move on. She would be faithful and rely on Him for her future, even if it meant singleness and being in lower social class as a widow and foreigner in a land. She would stay by Naomi's side until death.

Naomi and Ruth arrived in Israel during the barley harvest. Ruth went to the fields to glean the leftovers after the workers left to sell in the market for food.

The owner of the field, Boaz, took an interest in her story. Ruth let him know that he was her *kinsman-redeemer*. This Biblical term is used for a near relative who delivers, rescues, or redeems a person and/or their property (Leviticus 25:47-55, 27:9-25).

Boaz married Ruth. With her future secured, they had a son and cared for Naomi.

What appeared to be a hopeless situation turned out for the best. God had a plan for Ruth, and it resulted in a legacy for her and Naomi.

And a lineage that led to the birth of Christ! What an honor!

The outcome of this story reminds me of what Paul said in Ephesians:

> *"Now to him who is able to do far more abundantly than all that we ask or think, according to the power at work within us."* *(Ephesians 3:20)*

Ruth put the past behind her. She moved forward with courage and trusted in God's faithfulness for the future. And God did far more than Ruth could have ever asked or imagined.

When I accepted Christ as a young pre-teen, God put the Holy Spirit in me as a deposit and seal until I get to heaven (2 Corinthians 1:22). That Holy Spirit power is at work in us today. He is the same power that raised Jesus from the dead.

I had to put the recent past of my job change behind me so I could move forward to the plans God had in store for me. And when I released the past and I asked for His help, He gave me the ability to do more that I could ever ask or imagine in the days ahead.

When you experience a devastating change, the past can hold you in bondage when you think you can't hold your head up. You need to release it so you can look to the future.

There's hope ahead. God has bigger plans for where you are going, and they are more than you can ever ask or imagine.

Key: Replace the pull of the past with the hope of the future.

Read: Leviticus 25:47-55, 27:9-25; Ruth 1:16; Ephesians 3:20; 2 Corinthians 1:22

Action: What do you need to release from your past so you can look ahead to what is before you?

Prayer Moment: Lord, take my past. I don't need to keep dwelling there. I know You have a plan for me. I have hope because You will do more than I ask or imagine. Amen.

Section Two:

Humbly Give Yourself to Him and Release Your Pride

DAY ELEVEN

More of Him: Less of Me

"'He must become greater; I must become less.'"
John 3:30 (NIV)

I sang along with the song that played on the car radio. As I pulled into the store parking lot, I sat there listening and singing. And tears flowed down my face.

The song was *More of You* by Colton Dixon. The theme of the song is about how we focus on ourselves and need more of God as He is our everything.

Have you ever felt you so singularly focused on something that you knew you needed more of God?

Five weeks later after hearing this song, I was leading a women's Bible study on Proverbs when this verse struck me:

> *"The fear of the Lord is instruction in wisdom, and humility comes before honor."*   *(Proverbs 15:33)*

When I read it, I began praying the words and again tears rolled down my face. "Humble me Lord so I can have Your honor," I prayed.

My job was all-encompassing to me. It was stressful, and I felt like I was failing. Despite this stressful situation, I was proud of what I had accomplished in the twenty years I'd been at the company, and I wasn't ready to give up or go elsewhere.

But needing more of God and less of me had finally hit home to me. I had been chasing things in this world to honor me, and my pride was in the way. What the writer of Proverbs said about humility and honor had pricked my heart. What I needed most was God's honor. Nothing in this world could give me the satisfaction in this life that I was seeking.

It has been said that humility isn't thinking less of yourself but thinking of yourself less. We need to spend less time thinking our lives are all about us. Instead, we should zero in on the One who created us and knows us better than we do.

I find when I focus on God, pray, or do things for others, then the focus on me fades into the background.

The consuming thoughts about myself needed to be realigned with God and His plan for me. Each day is a balancing act of quiet time alone with God, completing necessary tasks to care for others, taking care of myself, and doing all these things to the glory of God.

The song I listened to and sang in the store parking lot ended with my surrendering to God and needing more of God.

Surrender to Jesus and humble yourself. Give Him everything that you are. He will lead you to what He desires you to be. Seek to have more of Him in your daily life and less focus on you.

Key: Replace your pride with humility. He will honor you for doing so.

Read: John 3:30; Proverbs 15:33

Action Plan: Think about the pride you have in your work and life. What prideful thought or action should you stop doing today? Turn that over to Him and replace it with humility.

Prayer Moment: Lord, I pray that You humble me so I can honor You. Take this pride that I have. I need more of You, Lord God, and less of me. Amen.

DAY TWELVE

No Pain, No Gain

"'My Father, if it be possible, let this cup pass from me; nevertheless, not as I will but as you will.'" Matthew 26:39

Working out is hard work. We sweat. We breathe hard and it may hurt. And we may even wish we were somewhere else. But when we complete the workout, we are glad it's over and we feel accomplished.

Maybe others love to workout. But for me, it is a challenge even getting started. Since hard work and pain is involved, it is much easier to sit back and do nothing. Binge-watching episodes on a streaming service, reading a book, or even mindlessly scrolling through my social media accounts sound more exciting than working out.

However, when we do nothing, this choice leads to consequences. We put on weight that affects our joints and our muscles get flabby. It affects our attitude. We become lethargic and feel down or depressed.

Our pain could be other things instead of exercise. It could be working at a job that is dissatisfying or a relationship that is filled with tension and strife.

Maybe like me you find it difficult to be motivated to do hard things, especially when there is effort involved or possible discomfort.

We need to humbly accept the pain that comes with our choices. All hard work involves pain. Choosing to not work on these challenging situations in our life comes with pain as well. One choice leads to accomplishment and satisfaction. The other leads to dejection and depression.

The choice is up to us. We can have a great outcome or the effects of inaction.

Since it can be a challenge to do something that we know will be painful or uncomfortable, we need to ask God for help. For example, if I'm finding it hard to work out consistently, I can ask God for His help.

Jesus is an example of humbly coming before God to ask for help. He told the disciples that He had sorrow in His heart. The thought of his impending death hurt so deeply. Then He asked them to pray while He prayed. After He walked away from them, He fell on his face to pray. There He humbly asked God if it were possible for the pain of the cross to be taken away.

"'My Father, if it be possible, let this cup pass from me; nevertheless, not as I will but as you will'" (Matthew 26:39).

He didn't ask for it to be temporarily averted but to be removed completely. Jesus asked with a humble attitude. Even though He was dreading the pain of the cross, He trusted God to do His will. For us to gain salvation, He needed to endure the pain and continue with God's plan. His pain was for our gain.

Your job situation or place in life may not be pleasant right now. It may be the minor pain of enduring a workout. Or it could be something more heartbreaking.

Whatever the pain, remember that with suffering comes sacrifice. We need to put our pride aside and humbly ask God for help to accept the pain and move on. When we do that, we gain His strength and endurance to continue.

Key: We need to humbly accept the pain that comes with the sacrifice and endure the pain to gain a better path.

Read: Matthew 26:36-39; Hebrews 12:1-2

Action Plan: What sacrifice do you need to make to replace the pride in your life? What pain do you need to accept as a result? Ask God for His guidance, and He will give you what you need to endure.

Prayer Moment: Lord, I am putting my pride down as I humbly come to you. I am asking you to help me to accept the pain. Thank you for giving me what I need to endure! Amen.

DAY THIRTEEN

Humble Benefits

"But he gives more grace. Therefore it says, 'God opposes the proud but gives grace to the humble.'" James 4:6

When looking for a new job, we may be looking for certain benefits. It could be healthcare for the family and a dental plan. There could be some intangibles you are looking for, like working from home. This may help you to work in peace and quiet away from a noisy cube environment.

What benefits do you look for in a new job? Are there some intangibles that you are hoping to get as well? You might find that your new job offers unexpected intangible benefits.

Prior to my job changing, I willingly dropped to my knees in humility. After I received the news of my job change and began the new job, my heart was a barren place with feelings of anger, regret, and shame.

I started the day by reading my Bible and praying each morning. But when the thoughts of these negative feelings nagged me throughout the day, I asked God to take them captive (2 Corinthians 10:5). They had no place being in my head!

In their place, God gave me many benefits to enjoy. He gave me the grace to speak respectfully of my old boss. Email questions would arrive in my inbox about my old position. As I stared at the blank page on my computer screen, He gave me the wisdom to reply with grace.

He gave me other advantages in this new season as well. In the morning, I have time to soak in God's Word and journal my prayers. My Christian boss is an encouragement to me. I work from home full-time so I can wear comfy clothes. Essential oils diffuse into the air and energize me or calm me. And Christian music plays on my phone and inspires me to do my job well as I continue with God's plan.

These are all intangibles I couldn't experience at the corporate office with noisy cubes and a scent-free environment. These benefits were blessings from being humbled. In this season of change for me, I had decided to take time to count the blessings instead of languishing for the old days or pining for what could have been.

This verse sums up this season's humble blessings:

"Oh, taste and see that the Lord is good! Blessed is the man who takes refuge in him." (Psalm 34:8)

David, the author of this psalm, found that when he took the time to count God's goodness, it was like savoring scrumptious food. He found blessings when he sought out God and dwelled in His presence.

Have you fallen to your knees in humility recently and are struggling to see His plan in your current struggles? Look around you and count the benefits that He has so graciously blessed you with at your job or in your life.

There are many benefits besides the ones listed in the job advertisement or your situation that you are not seeing. Ask God to open your eyes to see them and respond to Him with gratefulness.

Key: There are benefits and blessings to humility when we do His will.

Read: James 4:6; 2 Corinthians 10:5; Psalm 34:8

Action Plan: What unexpected blessings has God bestowed on you when you have been humbled recently? Thank Him today for those blessings!

Prayer Moment: Lord, open my eyes to see the benefits at my job. I thank you for each one right now. Amen.

DAY FOURTEEN

Unselfish Gain

"Do nothing out of selfish ambition or vain conceit but in humility consider others better than yourselves." Philippians 2:3

The sunrise came up each morning over the hills. The valley was lush with trees.

It was a beautiful place to be during the summer. Yet the work with the kids was tiring, and I was weary.

Working at a Christian camp for the summer can be so rewarding. They watch how you are kind, loving, and joyful. The younger kids give you hugs as they need that loving touch that they miss from their family members.

In quiet moments with them, you share about God and what He means to you. When they understand and believe in Jesus, you are blessed to be a part of their coming to God.

However, the long fifteen-hour days become physically draining. You wake up the next morning to repeat it again. The days off are a treasure so you can be recharged and continue the important work the next week.

Are you drained and weary from long days and the constant demands of others on your life? Do you feel like you are on a hamster wheel and not able to get off?

These Scripture verses were my memory verses for the summer:

> *"Do nothing out of selfish ambition or conceit but in humility count others more significant than yourselves. Let each of you look not only to his own interests, but also to the interests of others."* (*Philippians 2:3-4*)

God wants us to be selfless and think of others as more important than ourselves. And we are to do that with humility.

My focus was on serving the kids and adults that summer. I prayed often that God would help me love those around me with a humble attitude and that I would do nothing out of selfish ambition.

When I was weary and wanted to give up, God was my strength and my song. I learned about selfless ambition that summer.

When we truly serve others selflessly, we take ourselves out of the equation. The work isn't about us. The work becomes about those you serve. The people you serve and dedicate your time to each day are your customers, clients, vendors, employees/co-workers, or others in your life. They are there for you to love and care deeply about them.

Take a walk in their shoes for a moment and their needs as they walk into your restaurant, your hospital, your business, or come to your house. Then look at how you do your work or your attitude. What could you do better to serve them selflessly? Your customers or employees/co-workers will be well served and want to return when you have a humble and unselfish ambition to serve God and them.

When we focus only on our pain or our weariness, then we become single-minded. Our perspective is selfish, not other-centered. The work God has called us to do is important. Everyone has a customer to serve, a patient to care for, or a felt need to provide for those in their life.

When the sunrise comes up today, take the focus off you and zero in on those you are serving. You will gain more than a customer or a friend for life. You gain contentment from God by serving them selflessly.

Key verse: Live for God unselfishly and look out for others while still doing God's plan for your life.

Read: Philippians 2:3-4

Action Plan: What selfish tasks about your life can you put aside and serve others around you? Ask God for help to selflessly serve others instead of selfishly serving yourself.

Prayer Moment: Lord, what selfish ways should I remove to better serve You and others? Help me to see them as You do and serve them selflessly today and every day. Amen.

DAY FIFTEEN

Humble Dwelling

"'I dwell in the high and holy place, and also with him who is of a contrite and lowly spirit, to revive the spirit of the lowly, and to revive the heart of the contrite.'" Isaiah 57:15

Dust bunnies were everywhere. And the place needed to be cleaned up.

We have a janitor at our church who regularly cleans. But each spring our church members do a thorough sprucing up of our building and the property. There is a long list of special projects that need to be done, and we get busy checking off the list in a few hours.

But sometimes I don't want to be there. I don't like to clean, and sometimes cleaning is dirty work. There are tasks at home to complete or doing something fun with a friend would be more desirable.

Is cleaning your house at the top of your list of fun things to do?

Like all our houses, we should keep God's house polished up. When we do this special church cleaning day, the place looks brighter, and the clutter is gone. The sun shines brightly through the windows as the smudges have been removed. The building smells fresh and is ready for us to serve others again with a revived purpose.

Similarly, Paul wrote about our bodies being God's temple:

> *"Do you not know that your body is a temple of the Holy Spirit within you, whom you have from God? You are not your own, for you were bought with a price. So glorify God in your body." (1 Corinthians 6:19-20)*

Our bodies are where God lives. They are His temple. He dwells there when we have a humble heart that is focused on serving Him and Him alone.

In the disappointment of not being promoted at my job, I didn't have humility in my temple but had allowed pride to abide instead. I was jealous and angry about those who were promoted ahead of me. My heart was set on moving up the corporate ladder.

There isn't anything wrong with wanting to be promoted. But the problem was that I was trying to fill up the God-shaped hole in my heart with other things. Even though I knew Jesus as my Lord and Savior, I was searching for satisfaction in my work. I wanted to impress others with my significance.

Each morning I would read a few verses of Scripture and run off to work. I needed to spend time with God each morning to thoroughly clean my heart and be renewed in His presence. There were projects and clutter inside my heart that were piling up. I was cleaning my heart with a wet wipe, but it wasn't enough. My heart needed a spring cleaning.

What cleaning projects in your heart need to be washed, scrubbed, and polished?

We choose to put things into our lives or desire to go down a path that is contrary to God's ways. Like our houses, our hearts need regular cleaning. We need to spend time in God's Word to keep a clean heart and renewed Spirit within us (Psalm 51:20).

Don't wait for spring to do an inventory of what is in your heart and lurking in the corners. This is God's dwelling place. We need to spend time there in God's presence and clean it up today.

When those dust bunnies are removed from your heart and you are humbled before God, you will find a fresh perspective on what you need to do to honor Him. He breathes new life into you and your purpose is refreshed to humbly serve Him in the work you must do today.

Key: God dwells within those who are humble and contrite in heart.

Read: Isaiah 57:15; 1 Corinthians 6:19-20; Psalm 51:20

Action Steps:

What do you need to clean up in your heart to make it a humble dwelling for God? Ask God to forgive the dust bunnies in your life and make humility at home in your heart.

Prayer Moment: Lord, remove the dust bunnies, the sin, that is in my heart. I humbly come to You today to do the purpose you have given me. Help me to be humble as I serve those You put in my path. Amen.

Note: Does God dwell in your heart? If not, check out the Peace with God section in the appendix about having Him dwell within you.

DAY SIXTEEN

God Will Fight for You

"If possible, so far as it depends on you, live peaceably with all. Beloved, never avenge yourselves, but leave it to the wrath of God, for it is written, 'Vengeance is mine, I will repay, says the Lord.'" Romans 12:18-19

When our kids were little, we took them to a park to play. As the kids were playing, a couple of kids decided to pick on our daughter. Our son, who was four-years old at the time, stepped up to defend his older sister and told them to leave her alone. The bullies backed off. This is a great example of someone fighting for another and avenging them.

When my job changed, and I chose the position in another department. I was angry about not getting a promotion within my own department, and I wanted to seek out vengeance on those who had hurt me. But I needed to let God avenge me in His own time.

How about you? Have you been angry enough with someone that you'd like to take revenge on them?

In Romans 12, Paul tells us to never make a move and take revenge ourselves:

> *"If possible, so far as it depends on you, live peaceably with all. Beloved, never avenge yourselves, but leave it to the wrath of God, for it is written, 'Vengeance is mine, I will repay, says the Lord.'" (Romans 12:21)*

God will bring others to justice or punish them. Let God take care of it as it is His job. He has a timeline in which He will do it.

Instead of taking revenge on the other person, Paul tells us to live in peace with them. This means serving those who have hurt us. He ends the passage with:

> *"Do not be overcome by evil but overcome evil with good." (Romans 12:21)*

The Greek word for overcome, *nikao*, means to conquer, carry off, or be victorious.

We can't let our anger conquer us. Unrighteous anger is evil. But evil can be conquered by good.

Paul says that when we do good to those who are evil, it is like heaping burning coals on their head (vs.

20). Ouch! When a person is kind to the evil person, they cannot comprehend why a person would respond to them when they are being mean.

When I didn't get the promotion, I had hoped for within my department, I had a choice to leave my company or go to another department. Since I chose to stay, I needed to conquer my feelings of vengeance and leave it to God. Believing that God would avenge me was hard to do since I like to be in control.

However, God's timing allowed me to be around when He avenged me a year later.

We have all been in a place of anger and wanting to defend ourselves. The key is to calm down, be at peace with this person. Keep on serving the Lord and praying for His deliverance.

At the right time, God will avenge you like He did for me, and how our son did for our daughter.

Key: God is about justice. He avenges us when we live in peace and do good.

Read: Romans 12:18-21;1 Samuel 24

Action: What injustice have you been the victim of? God will avenge you and put it right. Ask Him to remove the anger, put it in the past, and help you to move forward.

Prayer Moment: Lord, I pray that You will avenge me. You know the timing and the day. I pray that You will help me to put my anger in the past, to live in peace, and do good to those around me. Amen.

Note: If you are being physically or emotionally abused, please seek help. No one deserves this treatment. You are precious to God, and He will provide for you!

DAY SEVENTEEN

His Humble Servant

"For am I now seeking the approval of man, or of God? Or am I trying to please man? If I were still trying to please man, I would not be a servant of Christ." Galatians 1:10

The new manager at work had been with the company for over twenty-five years in other departments but was now a manager. She asked a lot of good questions, and I thought I should get to know her and help her learn about being a manager of people.

Based on some other interactions with her, I had mixed feelings about her and decided to not pursue getting to know her.

A year later, after my job changed, I ended up taking the position in her department. It was humbling to think that I had at one time thought I could take her under my wing and teach her about being a manager.

However, she was teaching me how to do the work in her department now.

After I accepted the new job, I met with her to go over the job responsibilities and the program that I would be managing. She was excited to have me on her team because she wanted to learn from me.

It was a humbling experience.

Have you judged a person before and missed out on the joy of knowing them?

Paul wrote this to the believers in Galatia,

> *"For am I now seeking the approval of man, or of God? Or am I trying to please man? If I were still trying to please man, I would not be a servant of Christ." (Galatians 1:10)*

I was too busy trying to seek the approval of men and pleasing my former boss. This was not being a servant of Christ. Instead, I was prideful. And I was judging my new manager while missing out on the joy of knowing her as a person.

As I have gotten to know my new manager, I discovered she is a Christian and a servant to the team. She has been patient with me as I learned the new area. As I was healing from the hurt and the anger that I carried, she was compassionate and gave me grace.

And she asked me for advice in living out her Christian walk and studying the Bible. It has been such a joy to serve the Lord under her humble and insightful leadership.

When we are hurting, God knows exactly what we need and who we need to help bring us along. He has placed me under the guidance of this strong woman of God and at the same time has fulfilled my calling to write for Him. I couldn't do my daily work or write a single word without the help of God's power flowing through me (2 Peter 1:3).

Is God calling you to do something different? Are you humbly serving Him or are you trying to please others?

Listen and look for opportunities that God is opening to you. You may find the new manager, co-worker, or the next-door neighbor is the encouragement you need and is a humble servant of Christ.

Key: Be God's humble servant, stay true to what God has called you to, and you will have greater opportunities come your way.

Read: Galatians 1:10; 2 Peter 1:3

Action: How can you humbly serve others in your work today?

Prayer Moment: Lord, guide me to humbly serve You in my calling. Open my ears and eyes for opportunities to serve others so I don't miss the blessings You have waiting for me. Amen.

DAY EIGHTEEN

Prideful Reflection

"He will render to each one according to his works…. For God shows no partiality."
Romans 2:6,11

I love watching period dramas!

One of my favorites is *Pride and Prejudice*. The main character, Elizabeth, nearly misses out on love because she misjudged Mr. Darcy based on the stories of his treatment of others.

Have you judged someone by their appearance or attitude? Or maybe you didn't know their full story and jumped to conclusions like Elizabeth?

This movie reminds me of myself. I have judged what others have done or not done. An assumption is made based on their appearance or their attitude. But I don't know their heart, their hurt, or the pain they have suffered in their life. I have not walked a day in their shoes.

Unknowingly, I have put myself in God's seat to judge them. As I look in the mirror and see the self-righteous pride in myself, I need to let that go.

Thankfully, God has an entirely different point of view. God loves the people I'm judging, wants to know them, and desires a close relationship with them (1 Timothy 2:4). He views them with eyes of love and waits for them to choose Him.

God is watching to see what each person does and judges them with impartiality.

> *"He will render to each one according to his works…. For God shows no partiality."* *(Romans 2:6, 11)*

He doesn't look at a person's skin color, nationality, or gender. His interest is whether their heart is wholly devoted to Him and obediently serving Him.

I should not listen to what others say about people and make a judgment call based on their views. With humility, I need to listen to the truths of God's Word and how He sees them. He sees each person as loved, chosen, and precious. Each person that I encounter is made in the image of God, every single one.

Choose today to be different and put aside your prideful prejudices, like Elizabeth experienced in *Pride and Prejudice.* Determine to see others with the impartial eyes of the Lord.

Key: Prideful prejudice can be reflected two ways. Ensure you are on the humble side of the mirror.

Read: Romans 6:2; Romans 6:11; 1 Timothy 2:4

Action: Look in the mirror of your heart. What do you see in your reflection? What prejudice do you have of others that you need to put aside to love them instead? Ask God to remove that prideful prejudice and humbly see others as He sees them.

Prayer Moment: Lord, please remove the pride I have in my heart for those I know and don't know. Give me Your love to see them as You do. Amen.

DAY NINETEEN

Sufficient Ability

"Not that we are sufficient in ourselves to claim anything as coming from us, but our sufficiency is from God." 2 Corinthians 3:5

Have you ever made excuses for not doing something because you didn't know how, or you were afraid of failing?

I have done that. Many times.

Moses is a great example of this. God called Moses to be the person to talk to Pharoah about letting the Israelites leave slavery in Egypt. It was a monumental task to get a leader to free his slaves to go worship their God in their homeland and lose their free labor. But that wasn't what Moses was concerned about. He was worried about his capabilities for the job.

Moses asked God four different questions. He asked God if He was calling the right person. Secondly, he asked what he should say to the Israelites to convince them that God sent him. Then Moses wanted to know what to do if they didn't believe him and if God really called him. Lastly, he told God that he wasn't eloquent and was a slow speaker.

God patiently answered Moses. He said that He would be with Moses as he spoke to Pharoah. And when he talked with the Israelites, He said that Moses should tell them, "I AM sent me to you" (Exodus 3:11). He gave Moses the ability to do small miracles to convince them, like turning a staff into a snake and back again. And when made excuses about his speaking abilities, God said, "I will be with your mouth and teach you what you shall speak" (vs.12).

You'd think that would be enough to convince Moses. However, he told God to send someone else. Now God was angry, and His patience was wearing thin. He offered Moses' brother Aaron to go with him and speak to Pharoah for them.

Have you been asked to do a task and immediately turned the person down? Or peppered them with a lot of questions to clarify how you could get it accomplished? Or maybe you told them to give the task to someone else?

Or you may have said you aren't enough. And you end up in a full-blown pity party.

Here is something I learned recently. I am not enough by myself. I can't be enough without God.

The dictionary defines the word *enough* to mean "as much as required."

We aren't sufficient in ourselves to claim that anything we do comes from ourselves. It comes from the sufficiency we have in God.

> *"Not that we are sufficient in ourselves to claim anything as coming from us, but our sufficiency is from God." (2 Corinthians 3:5)*

The Greek word for sufficient is *hikanos* which means enough or sufficient in the ability or competency to meet or fit the requirements of the job.

Our being enough or enough-ability is in God alone. We need to quit making excuses about not being able to do it.

In whatever task that God is calling you to do, you can certainly ask questions to get clarity on the task like Moses did. But your yes to God's plan means that He will provide the "sufficient-ability" to do the job. If needed, like God did with Aaron, He will supply others to assist where specific skills may be required to complete the task.

Key: God will provide for you on the path and plan He has for you.

Read: 2 Corinthians 3:5; Exodus 3:1-14

Action: What excuses are you making to keep you from doing what God has called you to do? Put those excuses and lies behind you and believe you are enough because God says you are.

Prayer Moment: Lord, forgive me for the excuses I make for not doing the plan You have set out for me to do. With You, I have sufficient ability to do the tasks You have called me to do. You will provide the skills and resources to complete it. Amen.

DAY TWENTY

Thorny Roses

"My grace is sufficient for you, for my power is made perfect in weakness." 2 Corinthians 12:9

The pain in my hands was agonizing. It was sharp and deep in the thumb joint. I called to get a doctor appointment. I could see a medical doctor the next day, but an appointment with a specialist was two months out. The doctor determined that I had fibromyalgia and that started a journey of managing the pain.

Truthfully, I wasn't sure what I felt about this diagnosis. I was numb. The articles that I read online were not helpful. Some symptoms didn't add up, and I didn't have pain in all the areas that they said I should. The pain can vary between patients.

And the medication was frustrating. It would help me sleep well. However, the next morning I was in a fog and emotionally unable to make decisions at work for a few hours.

After one day of indecisiveness and crying, I told the doctor I didn't want to take the medication anymore. I went off the medications and managed my pain myself. I had already been using essential oils to reduce the pain topically. And I eliminated gluten from my diet, which reduced the inflammation in my body. These tactics were helping me cope with the pain. Without the medication, I could function mentally and be decisive at work.

Have you experienced pain that is debilitating or medication that is frustrating? Or have you received a diagnosis that has left you numb? What has helped you cope with the pain, frustration, and numbness?

Paul's words about his thorn in the flesh were helpful to me during this time. He had some type of physical issue that was causing him lasting pain. God had told Paul that His grace was sufficient or enough for him. God's power within him was made perfect in weakness.
Paul declared,

> *"When I am weak, then I am strong." (2 Corinthians 12:10)*

He had determined that if God got all the glory and God's power was perfected within him when he was weak, then he would be content with the hardships, the insults, and the suffering.

These weaknesses help us keep the focus on God and not ourselves. They humble us and prevent us from taking credit for the successes that we experience. And His power enables us to do more than we physically can when the pain has taken its toll.

These thorns in the flesh are like the thorns on roses. Thorns protect the plant from predators so they will continue to bloom and flourish.

We have thorns in our lives that protect us too. They keep us humble so that we aren't prideful in our life. God gives us His grace to persevere. The faith we have in Him allows us to go on despite the pain we endure.

Our life may appear rosy on the surface, but, on the inside, we are hurting from the ongoing thorns. Difficulties can be a daily occurrence, but we can bloom and flourish amid them. We gain strength from God in our life. His "sufficient-ability" gives us the capability to go on.

What is your thorn? Is it physical or emotional pain? Whatever thorns you have in your life, God's grace and power will keep you humble and keep you going throughout your day.

Key: Some thorns in life don't go away. They keep you humble. Rely on God for your strength to keep you moving forward.

Read: 2 Corinthians 12:9

Action: What is your thorn in your flesh? Thank God today for your thorns so you can humbly rely solely on Him for your strength.

Prayer Moment: Lord, thank you for my thorn I have in my flesh. I humbly come before You and rely on You for my strength. It is Your strength, not mine, that keeps me going. Amen.

DAY TWENTY-ONE

Relational Attitudes

"One of the criminals who were hanged railed at him, saying, 'Are you not the Christ? Save yourself and us!'" Luke 23:39

Two men hung on the crosses on each side of Christ. Their attitudes and words that day reflected the true content of their hearts.

One criminal challenged Him. He said if He was truly the Christ, why didn't He save himself and them?

This criminal, hanging on a cross and about to die, attacked Christ with a prideful attitude. He identified Jesus as Christ but asked about His identity in a rhetorical question. Then he mocked Him and asked why He didn't use His power to save them all.

The other criminal rebuked the man. He asked if he feared God because they were both hanging on crosses, condemned to die. Then he defended Jesus and said something that reflected his penitent heart:

"'We are receiving the due reward of our deeds; but this man has done nothing wrong.'

And he said, 'Jesus, remember me when you come into your kingdom.'" (Luke 23:41-42)

This second criminal realized that he was sinful and deserved the consequence of his deeds. He knew Jesus did not deserve this death. Then he asked for Jesus to remember Him once He got to heaven.

Two criminals. Two completely different attitudes.

Like these criminals, our mouths spew out what is inside our hearts. Matthew lists evil thoughts, murder, adultery, sexual immorality, theft, lies, and slander (Matthew 15:18-19). For most of us, these are not things that we'd even think of doing. But there are a few many of us have done. The one that sticks out to me is evil thoughts.

The word evil means wicked or bad. Many years ago, I was let go from a company and wanted to seek out revenge for the owner. I quickly repented of the evil thought.

That thought came from pride in my heart. I was defensive and was determined the other person understood the depth of the hurt they had inflicted on me. This attitude can hurt our relationship with others and with God.

The pride in our life does not come from God. He will not endure an arrogant heart (Psalm 101:5). This person seeks to inflate the opinion of themselves to gain attention. They focus on themselves instead of giving honor and glory to God.

How often do we display an attitude of pride that does not reflect Christ?

When thoughts of pride come, we need to humble ourselves before God and repent of them. Pride leads us down a path of destroying our soul. The more we gratify our sinful nature, the further we get from honoring God with our lives. This affects our relationship with Him as well.

Like the second criminal on the cross, come to God with an attitude of humility. This attitude will allow your time in His presence to be unhindered. Besides having precious time with our Lord, He will honor our humble attitude (Proverbs 18:12).

Key: Prideful attitudes hurt all our relationships, even our most important one with God.

Read: Luke 23:39-43; Matthew 15:18-19; Psalm 101:5; Proverbs 18:12

Action: What prideful attitude do you need to put to death? Thank Jesus for putting that attitude to death on the cross for you. Ask Him to give you a better attitude today that reflects Him.

Prayer Moment: Lord, I bring these prideful attitudes and lay them at Your feet. Thank you for taking them and putting them to death. Help me have an attitude of humility. May I glorify You in all I think, say, and do. Amen.

DAY TWENTY-TWO

Dead End

*"There is a way that seems right to a man,
but its end is the way to death." Proverbs 16:25*

Your friend drives up in a new car. It is shiny,

new, and your favorite color. Or friends go on the
perfect vacation to a warm, sunny beach while you're
stuck in cold weather. Your envy of them causes you
to be jealous, and you become resentful. Or maybe
you're living paycheck to paycheck with no extra
money to vacation.

Can you relate? I have thought these things many
times over the years.

Miriam, the sister of Moses, was jealous of her
brother who had a close relationship with God. He
spoke with God and his countenance glowed due to
being in God's presence.

Miriam spoke badly about Moses and judged him
because he had married a woman from Cush, a
foreign land to Israel. And she and their brother

Aaron spoke about how God talked to Moses and wondered why He only spoke to the people through him. Why couldn't God speak to them and through them as well? Weren't they important enough to be used by God as well?

> *"And they said, 'Has the Lord indeed spoken only through Moses? Has he not spoken through us also?' And the Lord heard it." (Numbers 12:2)*

We need to be careful what we think and speak. God knows our thoughts and hears our words. And if jealousy or pride is involved, He won't heed it. Pride can destroy a person and lead them down a path that leads to death.

Miriam and Aaron were on a slippery slope. God heard what they said and immediately asked to speak to them at the tent of meeting. He appeared in a pillar of cloud at the entrance. He told them how He spoke to prophets with dreams and visions. And with Moses, He spoke with clear words, which resulted in Moses glowing from being in God's presence.

The difference should have caused them to not question God. Moses had a closer and intimate relationship with God, which was like no other.

After God left their presence, Miriam was struck with leprosy. Even though Moses pleaded for her life, which God granted, she had to suffer from leprosy for seven days and live outside of the camp. While she sat in shame as an outcast outside the camp, Miriam had time to think about her words and her actions.

But with humility, a person gains wisdom. Miriam returned to camp with a restored body. Afterwards, they packed up their tents and moved on in their journey in the wilderness. I imagine that Miriam learned her lesson from speaking against Moses. Hopefully, she spoke words of wisdom and grace thereafter.

What about you? Is jealousy leading you down a slippery slope that leads to death?

The pride that I had in my work affected my health. I was on a slippery path and jealousy was leading me to a dead end. Instead, I humbled myself before God and He gave me a new path that restored me.

Our path can be a dead end, or it can be one that restores.

Key: Jealousy destroys; humility restores.

Read: Numbers 12; Proverbs 16:25

Action: What prideful way in your work needs to go? Ask God to humble you and remove what prideful ways need to be abandoned and lead you on the path He wants you to go.

Prayer Moment: Lord God, I humbly come before You and ask for You to remove any jealousy that's making me envious or prideful. Lead me to the path you want me to take to restore my soul. Amen.

Section Three:

Completely Trust Him for the Best Outcome

DAY TWENTY-THREE

Unbelief

"Cleanse out the old leaven that you may be a new lump, as you really are unleavened. For Christ, our Passover lamb, has been sacrificed."
1 Corinthians 5:7

There was a time when our family needed more income to pay bills as we were in debt and getting behind in making payments. All I could focus on was getting that needed income. Operating in unbelief, I interviewed for a job at a small company years ago. I ignored the red flags about the position and focused on the one thing I desired: the income I would receive. When I got an offer, I took it, thinking I'd found the answer to our problems.

One day out of frustration and anger, I complained about a situation at work to my boss. The next day, he let me go.

It wasn't my place to complain about what he'd done. My uncontrolled tongue resulted in job loss. In hindsight, God used my sinful mouth to escape that toxic situation, but I also learned a lesson about believing in God to provide.

While I cried out to God for direction during my time of unemployment, I relied on Him to provide for our needs. He led me to the company that I have been at for over 22 years. We have had a comfortable income to pay off our debts, get a house, and provide for the needs of our family.

Previously, I had chosen my own path. I didn't wait for God's timing and His provision. Ultimately, I didn't believe that He would take care of all our needs, including our debt.

Have you experienced this? Do you doubt God will provide for your needs and desires?

God wants to give us His best and perfect gifts. He makes a promise and doesn't change His mind about it.

> *"Every good gift and every perfect gift is from above, coming down from the Father of lights, with whom there is no variation or shadow due to change." (James 1:17)*

But we need to trust Him. We need to discard the unbelief that is hidden in our hearts.

This unbelief is like bad yeast that will take over a whole lump of dough. It will keep the dough from rising and becoming a loaf of bread.

"Cleanse out the old leaven that you may be a new lump, as you really are unleavened. For Christ, our Passover lamb, has been sacrificed." (1 Corinthians 5:7)

In 1 Corinthians, Paul is referencing the Feast of Unleavened Bread, which is a type of bread that the Jews ate for seven days during Passover. This was eaten in remembrance of when God saved the Israelites from slavery in Egypt. They ate unleavened bread and put the blood of a lamb on their doorposts so the angel of death would pass over their house, saving their firstborn sons (Exodus 12).

For Christians, Christ was the sacrifice for our sins. We need to be unleavened or unburdened from our old sins. In Christ, we are like a new lump of dough being formed with good yeast so we can live a full life of God's Spirit and truth.

Jesus said He is the bread of life (John 6:35). We need to live a life of godliness and His truth.

We need to throw out the unbelief and replace it with trust for the Almighty God who provides for our needs. He knows the path that we should take that will give us His best gifts.

Key: Rid yourself of unbelief and trust Him completely.

Read: James 1:17; 1 Corinthians 5:7; Exodus 12; John 6:35

Action: Review the path that you are on. Is it God's path? If it is not, what is one thing you can do to head towards the path He has for you?

Prayer Moment: Lord, forgive my unbelief. I trust You to lead me to Your path and the best gifts You have for me. Amen.

DAY TWENTY-FOUR

Restoration Business

"Therefore, if anyone is in Christ, he is a new creation. The old has passed away; behold, the new has come." 2 Corinthians 5:17

My husband loves watching television shows where they take a dilapidated house and turn it into a magnificent space. The transformed house is well decorated and extremely functional for the couples' living requirements. It is amazing to see how the worn down can be transformed into a new and exciting place for the family to enjoy their new home.

Much like changing and evolving old spaces into new ones, God is in the restoration business of changing and restoring lives. It is something He has been doing for centuries.

David was king of Israel and successful in winning battles. But he sinned and slept with Bathsheba, a married woman. He arranged for her husband to be at the front lines of the battle so he would be killed. Then he married Bathsheba and took her for his wife. Their child became sick and died because David's sin displeased the Lord. David repented of his sin and afterwards, he was able to defeat their enemies, the Ammonites, in battle (2 Samuel 11 and 12).

Peter denied Christ, not one or two but three times (Matthew 26:69-75). He repented and was restored as one of His faithful followers who preached the Gospel to many people who in turn believed in Christ (Acts 2:38-41).

These men were in a dilapidated state and in need of restoration. Maybe you're in the same place.

I was in a dilapidated state when I had an unplanned job change that took me out of my specific field of IS Security, a job that I had done for nearly twenty years. Despite how I felt like I failed in some ways, God was restoring my heart in working His plan for His glory. Not my plan for my glory.

During this time of restoration, I read a challenging devotional that talked about Peter's restoration. This quote sums it up: "Even after failure, Peter, returned to the Lord with a restored heart, stronger, more humble, ready for God to take him somewhere new" (www. barbpeil.com).

God has been changing and restoring me to take me somewhere new. Relaunching my blog and writing a book was the beginning for me.

What is dilapidated and broken in your life? What needs to be restored to a magnificent place where peace and purpose reside?

Through Christ, the old life can be torn down, and we can be restored and repurposed for God's plans for us.

"Therefore, if anyone is in Christ, he is a new creation. The old has passed away; behold the new has come." (2 Corinthians 5:17)

Seek out God to restore your stale heart and renew your life into something fresh. He has been waiting for you to come to Him – don't delay.

God desires you to place your trust in Him and restore your heart and life into something new. He has a new plan for you!

Key: God is in the Restoration Business. He can take the worn down and transform it into something beautiful again.

Read: 2 Samuel 11-12; Matthew 26: 69-75; Acts 2:38-41; 2 Corinthians 5:17.

Action Plan: What is one area in your life that God can begin restoring in you? Take a few minutes to talk that over with Him and ask Him for help.

Prayer Moment: Lord, tear down the old ways in my life that are in disrepair. I give them to You. Refresh me with Your plans and purpose You have for me. I wait with excitement for what You have for me. Amen.

Trustworthy Messages

"'The Lord of hosts, the God of Israel [had said]: Houses and fields and vineyards shall again be bought in this land.'" Jeremiah 32:15

Have you ever received a message from God

or how you will know it is from Him? Better yet, will you respond in obedience to do whatever He is asking you to do?

Jeremiah, a prophet in the Old Testament, got a message from God. He received prophesy that the kingdom of Judah would be overtaken. When he told King Zedekiah this information, he was thrown into prison.

While in prison, Jeremiah received a second message to buy a plot of land. This message would come from his cousin, Hanamel. His uncle, Hanamel's dad, was being forced to sell his land and the law allowed the land to be sold to a relative to keep it in the family (Leviticus 25:23-28).

Hanamel visited him in prison and said the exact words from Jeremiah's dream! Since the prophetic dream happened exactly as God had said, Jeremiah knew the message was from God and it was trustworthy (Jeremiah 32:1-8).

Even though it was a time of war and buying the property wouldn't have been a wise investment, Jeremiah responded in obedience. He did what God told him to do. He bought the land, signed the deed, and put a copy in a clay jar for safekeeping to give to Baruch, his scribe. (Jeremiah 32:9-14).

When he gave it to Baruch, Jeremiah said,

> *"The Lord of hosts, the God of Israel [had said:] 'Houses and fields and vineyards shall again be bought in this land.'" (Jeremiah 32:15)*

God had a plan for this land. Judah would be restored back to the land, and they would prosper there once again.

Like Jeremiah, I received a message from God, and I knew it was trustworthy.

After my position was eliminated and I made the decision to take the other position within the company, I took a few days off and spent time with my daughter and the grandkids.

The night before I left her house, I was regretting my decision about the other position and my spirit was downcast. As I was driving home, I was considering taking the severance option to leave the company instead.

My phone notified me that I had a text message, so I listened to it on my car radio through Bluetooth.

I immediately called my friend who sent me the text to confirm the message was real. I let her know that I was driving and couldn't respond. Could she please repeat that again?

She said, "My neighbor had a dream about you. She called me this morning to tell me about this message from God and asked if it made sense.

> 'Stay the course because His hand is all over this. He has big things for you.'"

My friend asked again, "Does this make sense to you?"

"Yes!" I exclaimed. "Last night, I was regretting my decision to take the new position. I didn't sleep well and was calling out to God. As I was heading home today, I was planning to call Human Resources and ask if I could take the severance instead. This message means that God doesn't want me to do that. He wants me to stay and work in this new position!"

Unlike Jeremiah, I didn't know that this message was coming but the content aligned with the plans I had for that day. God's message rescued me from a destructive path that could have ended in long-term unemployment. God is good!

Are you staying in close contact with God and listening for messages from Him? He wants what is best for us. We can trust Him with the best plan and path for us.

Key: God gives us special messages when it is important to stay on His path and plan.

Read: Jeremiah 32:1-15; Leviticus 25:23-28

Action: Be watchful and listen for God's messages to you and be obedient to do them.

Prayer Moment: Lord, I thank you that You give messages to Your children to act upon them. Help me to listen for Your instructions and be obedient to do whatever You ask of me. Amen.

Painful Trust

"Then they spit in his face and struck him. And some slapped him, saying, 'Prophesy to us, you Christ! Who is it that struck you?'" Matthew 26:67-68

The pain was unbearable. It stretched down my back. How much longer would this pain go on? I had to keep breathing through the pain.

Yet it only lasted for a short while and our beautiful baby boy was born.

Whenever we endure pain, we wonder if it will ever quit and how we can continue. Yet sometimes pain can go on for years. The prophet Jeremiah asked God why his pain was unceasing and why God was refusing to heal him (Jeremiah 15:16).

When my pain was intense, it didn't seem like the pain would be brief. However, many women before me had children and survived. I trusted that I would make it through and hold a baby soon. I am so thankful my pain was brief and resulted in a baby to hold, snuggle, and raise up to love Jesus!

Have you endured unbearable pain? Did you trust God to get you through that pain to a better outcome?

Jesus endured such pain as well. He had been ridiculed and stones were thrown at Him. The Jews did not like that He called himself God (John 10:31-33). Mockery was part of His pain.

> *"They spit in his face and struck him. And some slapped him, saying, 'Prophesy to us, you Christ! Who is it that struck you?'" (Matthew 26:67-68)*

After being arrested and sentenced to die on a cross, He was beaten. The whip was made with embedded pieces of bone and metal on each of the many tentacles.. The ends of the whip tore into Jesus' flesh with each swing. It typically took forty lashes to kill a person. However, the Romans would beat a person thirty-nine times, so he'd remain alive, writhing in pain.

Once Jesus was beaten, He was forced to carry His cross to a hill, called Golgotha, or the Skull, where the crucifixion took place. Railroad-like spikes were hammered between the bones in His hands and feet to adhere Him to the cross. He labored to breathe as the gravitational pull and weight of His body was suffocating His lungs. It was a long and grueling death.

However, it was God's will for Jesus to bear the weight of all the sins of the people in the world. Jesus trusted God for the outcome, and He trusted God while going through the pain, for all of us!

Whatever pain we are dealing with today, we need to trust God that there is a bigger plan beyond the pain. We need to wait patiently for what God has in store for us. Even though the pain may be unbearable at times, we need to trust Him for the outcome. We need to exercise painful trust.

Key: Endure the painful suffering you're encountering and trust God for the outcome.

Read: Matthew 26:67-68; John 10:31-33; Jeremiah 15:16

Action: Give the pain over to God today. He knows and understands the suffering you are enduring. If you aren't enduring pain today, pray for those who are.

Prayer Moment: Lord, I give You my pain today. You understand my suffering. Help me to endure it and trust You for the bigger plan beyond the pain. Amen.

DAY TWENTY-SEVEN

Trusting Benefits

"Give thanks in all circumstances; for this is the will of God in Christ Jesus for you."
1 Thessalonians 5:18

I n my teenage daughter's eyes, everything had gone wrong at school that day.

"How could those girls treat me that way? And the test that I studied so hard for in history, I got a C!"

The list went on and on about how awful her day had been. She was upset and needed someone to listen to her.

After letting her talk for a while, I told her that I wanted her to think back about her day and tell me three things that she was thankful for.

I wanted her to have a grateful attitude. Even when it seems like everything adds up to a bad day, there are always things to be thankful for.

Have you had one of those days where it seems like everything went wrong or the day was upside down? I have had them too. All I want to do is complain!

Instead, God wants us to be thankful. It is His will for us to be thankful all the time.

> *"Give thanks in all circumstances; for this is the will of God in Christ Jesus for you."*
> *(1 Thessalonians 5:18)*

When we give thanks, we are blessed. We receive this blessing from having a new life in Christ. We put our trust in God and believe what He has ahead for us is in our best interest. The benefits we receive by trusting Him are more than we can count.

The blessings or benefits come in many ways. When we are more thankful for things, people, or abilities we have, our perspective changes. We look upward and outward, instead of inward.

What do we see around us that causes us to pause and be thankful for all He has done and given us? Who needs my help or encouragement? How is God blessing me in this season of my life that I need to keep focusing on His benefits rather than what I don't see is right in my world?

These benefits allow us to trust that God has something more for us. There may be a lesson we can learn from the current situation. A friend who needs our encouragement. Or something new that fits the purpose that God has for us. We need to trust Him that whatever new experience He has for us outweighs the pain or agony we are currently facing (2 Corinthians 4:16-18).

The other day, my adult daughter called me. She said, "Mom, you'd be proud of me. I went out for dinner with some girlfriends who were complaining about their situations. After listening for a while, I told them I wanted them to think about their circumstances, and list three things that they were thankful for."

I smiled.

Thankfulness is to be practiced and done in all circumstances. It is God's will for us to be thankful.

Key: Give thanks, look for the benefits in all circumstances, and trust God that He has the best outcome for you.

Read: 2 Corinthians 4:16-18; 1 Thessalonians 5:18

Action: Thank God for three benefits you are enjoying right now in your life.

Prayer Moment: Lord, when I am having a bad day, remind me to be thankful because that is Your will for me. Help me to trust You because You have been faithful to me, and I have Jesus in my life. Amen.

Trusting Focus

"Trust in the Lord with all your heart, and do lean not on your own understanding. In all your ways acknowledge him and he will make straight your paths." Proverbs 3:5-6

Glasses can be a pain. I have worn glasses or contacts since I was a kid. But they are necessary for having things in focus and seeing what is ahead of you.

When I was young, I wanted glasses. My mom would ask why I was sitting so close to the television, and I would tell her that it was so I could get glasses. Weird, right? She rolled her eyes and told me to move back from the screen. But a few years later, things far away were getting blurry for me. My wish to get glasses had been granted.

In high school, I loved it when I got contacts. I didn't need spectacles attached to my face every day. I could pop the contacts in my eyes in the morning and remove them later that night. Problem solved!

As I aged, I needed bifocals and had to wear readers with my contacts. The glasses came on and off throughout the day for words to be in focus. It was irritating. But whenever I wore my glasses or contacts, everything was in focus.

Do you have glasses or contacts? Or were you blessed with twenty/twenty vision? Whether we have glasses or perfect vision, we don't know what is on the plan for us next week, month, or the years ahead.

There are so many times that I have tried to understand what God was telling me. I wasn't patient enough to wait and listen for God's answer so I would forge my own path. When I choose my own way, I have encountered problems, and my anxiety increases. I turn to God, and He lets me know that the path I am walking or running down is not safe.

I have learned to lean on God and trust Him for the path that I need to be on. When I trust Him, then the path in front of me is clear or in focus.

These verses in Proverbs are some of my favorite verses.

> *"Trust in the Lord with all your heart, lean not on your own understanding. Acknowledge Him in all your ways and He will make straight your paths."* *(Proverbs 3:5-6)*

My focus needed to be realigned to a spiritual focus. That focus needed to be from a totally different viewpoint. My view is near sighted, and I can't see far away. I can only see what is in front of me, but I don't know what is ahead.

God does. He knows what I will need on the path ahead. If the path is going to veer off abruptly, I will need His insight. That means I need to acknowledge Him.

We need to be aware of His presence in all our ways. We need to communicate with Him and see what new adventure or path we should take.

When we put our spiritual glasses on, we can begin to see the path from His viewpoint. God will shine a light ahead on the path, just enough for you to see where you need to go (Psalm 119:105).

Key: Put on your spiritual glasses and focus on God's point of view, not yours.

Read: Proverbs 3:5-6; Psalm 119:105

Action: What is God's point of view of your current work or life situation? Review it with Him and ask Him for help in leaning on Him for the straight path you should be on.

Prayer Moment: Lord, help me to trust You and put aside my understanding of my path. I acknowledge You today. Give me Your spiritual focus and light to see the straight path in front of me. Amen.

DAY TWENTY-NINE

Your Red Sea Miracle

"'The Lord will fight for you and you have only to be silent.'" Exodus 14:14

The situation seemed hopeless. I cried out to God because I was frustrated with one of my employees. Should I switch fields? In my prayers, I let God know about my questions and doubts about being in this position. But I persisted. I needed to be diligent in being a better manager, so I attended graduate school to improve my management skills.

Have you been in a situation that seemed hopeless? And like me you wondered if you should give up? There is hope.

Much like me, the Israelites had been crying out to God about needing a change in the way things were currently going. They were slaves in Egypt. The work was burdensome under the slave masters. They called out to God for help.

After being called by God through a fiery bush, Moses enters the scene and lets the people know that the Lord had heard their cries. He would lead them out of Egypt to the Promised Land. However, Pharoah wouldn't relent in letting the people go worship their God in the wilderness.

Due to Pharaoh's hardened heart, God sent ten plagues upon the Egyptians so they would know that He is the Lord. After the tenth plague, the death of Pharaoh's first-born son and many others' first-born sons throughout the land, the Israelites were allowed to go. The Israelites were given jewels and clothing from their neighbors to take with them, like God had told them they would do. Six thousand men plus women and children left Egypt on foot (Exodus 12:36-37).

Pharaoh's heart was hardened again, and the Egyptians began pursuing the Israelites who were camped by the Red Sea. They were afraid and asked Moses why he had brought them out there to die. He told them to not fear and that they would see the salvation of the Lord and not be harmed by the Egyptians. Then he said this:

> "'The Lord will fight for you and you have only to be silent.'" (Exodus 14:14)

God moved the pillar of cloud to behind them and the Egyptians were in darkness to keep them from reaching the Israelites. Then Moses stretched out his hand over the sea and the water receded, so the people walked on dry land and crossed safely to the other side! The Egyptians followed, and Moses moved his hand back over the water, causing all the Egyptians to drown (Exodus 14:21-28).

The Israelites had been rescued by a Red Sea miracle that day! They didn't have to do a thing to fight the Egyptians, other than walk on the dry ground that God provided.

God had heard their cries and provided. And He heard my cries and provided for me as well. The changing of my job and providing another job was my Red Sea miracle.

The Lord hears us when we cry out in hopelessness to Him, and He responds. His timing may not be our timing, but it will come at the exact right time. While you wait for your Red Sea moment, keep trusting God has a plan and He will bring it to fruition at the right time.

All you need to do is be silent. He will do the rest.

Key: Trust God's plans while you wait for your Red Sea miracle to lead you to your next steps.

Read: Exodus 12:36-37; Exodus 14

Action: Pray about your situation and the Red Sea miracle that you are waiting for and believe that His plan is the best one for you.

Prayer Moment: Lord, I pray there will be an end to my hopeless situation. I trust You and believe that You will perform a Red Sea miracle for me. You have the best plan for me, and I believe You will do it. Amen.

DAY THIRTY

Hopeful Plans

"'For I know the plans I have for you,' declares the Lord, 'plans for welfare and not for evil, to give you a future and a hope.'" Jeremiah 29:11

The job seemed perfect. It was in my field of IT Security. Even though it was across the cities, there was a possibility of working remotely. My contact there said it was a good company to work for, and they had a good reputation.

In my previous position, I had been interviewing potential candidates for over ten years. But now it was my turn to be the interviewee. Scared was not the word for it. I was overwhelmed with anxiety and sweating as I cringed in fear about going to this interview. Why was I so afraid? My underlying fear of failure was coming to the surface. I had to snap out of this fear and reframe my viewpoint from the other side of the table.

Has anxiety or worry been so high that you were sweating, and your heart rate was beating fast? Do you worry about the future and whether your plans will come together?

To bring my anxiety down about the interview, I had to set the worries aside and take a logical approach. I researched the top ten interview questions and wrote down all the answers. I reviewed the technologies that the company was implementing. And most of all, I prayed that God would give me the words to say and be at peace throughout the process.

The Lord kept me at peace during the interview. However, ten minutes into it, I knew that this wasn't the job for me. After this interview experience, I knew I could get through the interview process if I found another position that was a good fit for my skills and interest.

I had hoped that this job was potentially the one to keep me in the IT Security field that I loved. A couple of months later, my contact at the company messaged me that the boss I would have had was bad. He said it was a good thing I didn't get the job there.

God protected me from going into a situation with an unpleasant supervisor. He knew that staying in the current job that I had was far better than anything that I was searching for.

> *"'For I know the plans I have to you,' declares the Lord, 'plans for welfare and not for evil, to give you a future and a hope.'" (Jeremiah 29:11)*

God's plans are better for us. His plans are for our welfare. The Hebrew word for welfare in this verse is *shalom*. It is defined as completeness, soundness, or peace. He wants us to be content with what we do and feel secure in who we are in Him. The work itself is a means to an end. Besides caring about our essential needs, He wants us to live in contentment.

There may be chaos in your life, or you are in a seemingly hopeless situation. Knowing that God has a plan to give us a future and hope, we can have a different perspective on the circumstances. We know that they are temporary, and we can look forward to a better plan. Ultimately, we can look forward to the future hope He has promised us in Heaven.

Key: God has plans that give us hope for the future and perspective on the chaos.

Read: Jeremiah 29:11; Romans 5:3-5

Action: Think of an example of where God had a better plan for you than what you planned and thank Him for sparing you from that situation.

Prayer Moment: Lord, thank you that even when there is chaos, there are better things ahead. I am thankful God and hopeful because You have a better plan of hope for me. Amen.

No Fear Zone

"And walking in the fear of the Lord and in the comfort of the Holy Spirit, [the church] multiplied." Acts 9:31

There are riots, earthquakes, tornados, forest fires, and virus threats all around us. During the pandemic of 2020, we were stuck in our houses and not able to live life as we knew it. The fear overwhelmed us.

Have you lived in fear sometime in your life? Was that fear overwhelming to you?

The disciples lived in a time where they were being persecuted by a sect of Jews called the Pharisees. That fear had to be overwhelming. One man who consistently attacked them and yelled evil threats at them was Saul. He was a learned man who had studied the Old Testament laws and God's Word.

Saul came to know Christ and started preaching about Jesus. The disciples were amazed at first and thought he was tricking them. But Saul kept on proving that Jesus was the Christ.

Soon the Jews saw Saul as a threat and wanted to kill him too. Barnabas defended Saul and explained how he had come to Christ. After that, the disciples helped Saul by putting him on a boat to Tarsus (Acts 9:1-31).

There was peace in the church, and it began to grow. This was due to them

> "*walking in the fear of the Lord and the comfort of the Holy Spirit.*'" (Acts 9:31)

The disciples were relying on God. They knew that He would bring about good things from the persecution that was happening. Jesus had called them to follow Him and share the Gospel about Him being the Messiah to save people from their sins. As a result, the people had peace during the chaos and shared their faith with others around them. And the church grew by thousands.

God can do the same for us today. We can put our fears aside so we can quit living in the "fear zone." That is not healthy, and, honestly, it can be downright depressing. God is above all things, even the chaos around us. He knows what's going on and is in control (1 Chronicles 29:10-13). He can stop all that is going on and bring those to justice who are rebelling against His authority. But this may not be the right time. We are on God's timeclock.

In the meantime, we need to obediently fear the Lord and wait. Fearing the Lord means to have a reverential respect of Him. The Father knows the time when Jesus will return for the believers (1 Thessalonians 4:13-18), and when He will bring about justice for the evil one and the unrighteous.

> *"And we know that for those who love God all things work together for good." (Romans 8:28)*

When we know Jesus as our Lord and Savior, we can rely on God's strength to get us through the fires, the floods, and everything else that comes our way. And we can be comforted by the Holy Spirit that He gave us as a deposit. He will guide us and protect us.

Life with God can be a time of peace. We can exist in His peaceful living zone. And help multiply the church while we wait for the return of Jesus.

Key: The no-fear zone is a peaceful living zone with God.

Read: 1 Chronicles 29:10-13; Acts 9:1-31; Romans 8:28; 1 Thessalonians 2:13-18

Action: What fears do you need to put aside today and trust God that He will work it all out for your good?

Prayer Moment: Lord, help me put my fears aside. You are in control of the whole earth. You have a plan for when You will rescue believers and bring about justice. Thank you for the peace that I have in You. Amen.

DAY THIRTY-TWO

Satisfaction

Cravings

"Satisfy us in the morning with your steadfast love, that we may rejoice and be glad all our days." Psalm 90:14

The cookie was calling my name. After taking a bite, the warm, gooey chocolate oozed out of it. I knew that I wanted to eat it. But I didn't really need it either. After all, I had sampled others from the first two batches that came out of the oven.

That is the way it is with most food that I crave and can't wait to eat. It tastes so satisfying when I first eat it. But afterwards, that satisfying feeling goes away and my stomach feels bloated. I should not have eaten the last two cookies.

Have you sampled cookies from each batch out of the oven? They are so good when they are warm.

Are there other foods or things in this life you try to satisfy your cravings with?

Solomon said,

> "*All the toil of man is for his mouth, yet his appetite is not satisfied." (Ecclesiastes 6:7)*

We work so that we can fulfill our needs of food, clothing, and shelter. But when we seek to find our satisfaction in them, we'll find that they do not bring us the contentment we desire.

Many strive after money. Yet this doesn't satisfy us either. Solomon determined that

> "*He who loves money will not be satisfied with money, nor he who loves wealth with his income; this also is vanity." (Ecclesiastes 5:10)*

I have craved food, money, and promotion within the company I worked at. I worked long hours to finish strong and get ahead. My sleep was affected and my health as well. Solomon came to the same conclusion that the way we do business in this world leads to a lack of sleep (Ecclesiastes 8:16).

Besides having the comforts of living, one of our basic needs is for acceptance. Work becomes one of those areas in our life where we want to excel and find the approval we desire. Once we do well at our job and others are pleased with our work, we have satisfaction in what we do. However, working to satisfy ourselves can become an idol if our work is not kept in the proper perspective.

God provides for us and gives us what we need. And we can enjoy our work. Solomon calls this a gift from God to be happy with our work and what we do. We become so preoccupied with our work that we don't keep track of the days, and God gives us a joyful heart (Ecclesiastes 5:18-20).

The psalmist asked God to

> "*Satisfy us in the morning with your steadfast love, that we may rejoice and be glad all our days." (Psalm 90:14)*

The Greek word for steadfast is *hesed* which means goodness, kindness, and faithfulness. Knowing that God loves us with a love that is good, kind, and continuous is enough for us to be happy with what we do. Doing our work for God and His glory can bring us the contentment that we desire. That contentment allows us to rejoice and be glad daily in what we do.

Our satisfaction doesn't need to come from a chocolate chip cookie, a perfect body, a gorgeous house, or what status we achieve at work. It comes from God alone, and we can rejoice in our work for all our days.

Key: Satisfaction comes from God, not from who we see in the mirror or what we want to become in life.

Read: Ecclesiastes 5:10,18-20; Ecclesiastes 6:7; Ecclesiastes 8:16; Psalm 90:14; Colossians 3:23-24

Action: Determine today your satisfaction will be in God. What is one change you will make towards being satisfied in Him?

Prayer Moment: Lord, remove my desires for all these other things that don't satisfy me. Please satisfy me with Your steadfast love so I can rejoice in my work and be content all my days. Amen.

Section Four:

Waiting for Him to Reveal His Immeasurable and Unimaginable Plan

Steps Planned Out

"The heart of man plans his way, but the Lord establishes his steps." Proverbs 16:9

Each week I have a plan for what needs to be done. I use an application to schedule meals that I can access on all my devices, including my shopping list. My steps, hours that I stand during the day, and minutes of exercise are all tracked. My husband jokes that I have a plan and a spreadsheet for everything.

Sometimes I wish that were true. When I have a plan and everything gets checked off, I feel accomplished. I feel like I can conquer the world. But that is not the case. There are still things that I want to achieve. And there are things like dusting that don't get done as often as it should. And washing windows—what is that?

Do you have your life planned out? What things are important for you to plan out? And what do you let go? Do you get upset when your plans don't work out?

With these plans, I need to leave room for spontaneity and fun. When I do that, it leads to great memories that I share with my family and friends. No one remembers the detailed plan that I put together. They remember the moments of fun together, laughing, and playing.

If the plan doesn't happen the way I envisioned it, then I am upset, disappointed, and mad. Why shouldn't the plan go as I expect it to?

Because I am not God and the sovereign One in control of everything. We may plan but God is the one that sets our steps into place.

> *"The heart of man plans his way, but the Lord establishes his steps." (Proverbs 16:9)*

In the Hebrew, the heart, "*leb*," means the mind, will, heart, and understanding. Your desires, emotions, character, and conscience start from your heart. Everything begins at the center of your being.

You may be wondering what role your brain has here. Doesn't the idea begin in your brain? You may have an idea to do something, but that desire comes from your heart.

Jesus said,

> *"'For from within, out of the heart of man, come evil thoughts, sexual immorality, theft, murder, adultery.'" (Mark 7:21)*

The list of sins continues but Jesus' point is everything starts from the heart, even our thoughts and ideas. They all have a beginning, whether good or bad, where they are conceived, said, and done.

Plan, or "*chasab,*" means to think, invent, devise, imagine, or consider. We make plans for what we consider to be the best way to do something.

Direct or establish, "*kuwn,*" means to set up, to arrange, or direct toward. Whatever we think or devise, the Lord will direct us to what is the best for us. We aren't forced to go with His plans as He always gives us a choice.

We need to trust that He has the best interest for us. The world is not going to fall apart because one of our plans doesn't precisely go the way we want it to. We must let go of failed plans, ideas, or inventions and trust God for His plan. We don't know when these planned steps may happen. But God is faithful, and He will direct our steps to what is best for us.

Key: Let God give us His plan even for our daily steps.

Read: Proverbs 16:9; Psalm 37:23

Action: Do you plan everything out about your day? What is one area where you could trust God for your steps?

Prayer Moment: Lord, I give my plans to You. I need Your wisdom to make decisions that honor You. I trust You to direct my steps today. Lead me to the best plan You have for me. Amen.

Open Ears

"And now, oh sons, listen to me:
blessed are those who keep my ways."
Proverbs 8:32

I remember when we brought our baby daughter home from the hospital. We were in awe of how God beautifully formed her, and her little fingers and toes were so cute. And, like any new parents, we were anxious about her welfare.

We'd lay her down in her crib for a nap. If she made a slight sound, we'd rush in to see if she was okay. Our ears were propped open and primed to listen for a whimper, a cry, or a grunt. We poured ourselves into her care and had an open ear for her cry.

Like my husband and I listening to every sound that our baby girl would make, we need to keep our ears attentive to God's messages so we can receive His instructive wisdom.

After my job transition, I immersed myself in God's Word and poured my heart out to Him. When I sat down and scrolled through social media, the Bible verses that Christian authors and writers posted brought God's healing balm to my hurting heart.

I would go on walks and listen to podcasters. God's Word and His truth were being communicated through these speakers.

Wherever I turned, God was using friends at church, at work, and posts on social media to get my attention.

It was working, and I was listening. He had gotten my attention. Did a shocking and gut-wrenching change need to happen for God to get my attention? Yes, it needed to happen that way.

Have you had a hard or trying situation where God was trying to get your attention? Sometimes life is hard, and we try to figure it out. We wonder what we can learn from this situation.

But does God need to use these trying times to get our attention? No, it doesn't need to be that way. We can choose to open our ears and look around us. One question we can ask ourselves is, "What is God telling me today?"

> *"Listen to advice and accept instruction, that you may gain wisdom in the future."*
> *(Proverbs 19:20)*

The Hebrew word for listen or hear is "*shama*" which means to listen with intention or yield to in obedience.

We need to intentionally open our ears to hear what God is instructing us to do. And we need to accept or receive what He is telling us.

When we decide to look around and open our ears to God's instruction, we learn lessons we can apply in the future. We become wiser and know what to do when the next trial comes our way.

Solomon recorded these words in Proverbs.

> *"And now, oh sons, listen to me: blessed are those who keep my ways." (Proverbs 8:32)*

God is leaning over and telling us to listen and follow His path. When we do, we are richly blessed.

Like an ear perked up to listen for your baby's cries, we need our ears open to hear the messages God intends specifically for us.

Key: Listen for God's messages from various sources all around you.

Read: Proverbs 8:32; Proverbs 19:20

Action: What is one thing you can do today to listen with your ears open to God's messages around you? Then keep doing it. Listen and see how God is speaking to you.

Prayer Moment: Lord, help me to open my ears and listen for You speaking to me. You are surrounding me with Your Word, and You know what I need to hear.

DAY THIRTY-FIVE

Other Focused

"The effective prayer of a righteous person has great power." James 5:16

I was having a down day. My troubles were few, but I was recounting them repeatedly in my head. This replication in my brain had put me into a pit of despair.

Then I remembered my friend who was lying in the hospital in pain with cancer that was ravaging her body. I called out to God on her behalf and prayed for her healing, that He would heal her according to His will. Remove the pain as He saw fit to do so. And encourage her with the note I had sent days before.

Praying for her led me to pray for others in our church body who were ill. Or friends at work or neighbors who needed to hear about the grace that God has given us through new life in Christ.

The cloud of despair was lifting from my soul as I put my focus on those around me who had far greater needs than I. As I prayed for them, it reminded me of all that God had done for me. I lifted my heart up in praise to God for His provision for me and my family.

Have you had a pity-party sort of day? How do you escape that pit?

When I am down and having a pity-party or waiting on God for my next place of His promise for me, the best remedy is to pray for others and do something to encourage them.

In James 5:13-16, we read instructions about when to pray and the effect of prayers said in faith. James says to pray when people are suffering. Give praises when they are cheerful. And when someone is sick, they should ask the church elders to come and pray over them. James concludes,

"The effective prayer of a righteous person has great power." (James 5:16)

The word effective in Greek means to put forth power. It is the power of the Holy Spirit that lives in us to pray and call on Him to work in our lives and the lives of others. Those who are righteous and keep God's commands are the ones who have this ability of effective prayers. These prayers accomplish much for the Kingdom of God.

Think about all the times when you provided a meal for a family that brought home a new baby or had a death in the family. Or the time you provided a ride for an elderly person. Maybe you sent a card to encourage a friend. These good works allow you to feel happy that you were able to help another person.

Praying for others and being focused on their needs evokes those same feelings.

When your focal point shifts from being self-absorbed to other-focused, then the pity-party blues fly away.

Who do you need to pray for or encourage today?

Key: Being other focused takes the focus off you.

Read: Proverbs 15:29; James 5:13-16

Action: Look around you. Who needs encouragement today? Pray for a friend or loved one. Send them a card. Or call them on the phone and pray with them.

Prayer Moment: Lord, when I am feeling down, help me to lift my head up to You and focus on the needs of others. Let me know who needs Your encouragement today. Amen.

Good Medicine

"A joyful heart is good medicine, but a crushed spirit dries up the bones." Proverbs 17:22

There are times in our life when we seem to dwell in the valley and roads are rough. We long for the days when we were on the mountain top and loving life. But it is in the valley where we call out to Him and soak up all the dew that He sends us in the morning.

Have you experienced tough times too? What Bible verses have encouraged you during that time? Who came alongside you to support you through those tumultuous waters?

When my job had changed and I was navigating the new path God had put me on in the new position, I spent time in God's presence each day — praying and reading His Word. But I also had friends who shared their concern and words of wisdom with me.

The friends who spoke God's Word to me and encouraged me were precious. They were like dew that gave me nourishing strength from His Word.

They were sharing God's love with me in a time of need.

These friends exemplify what Solomon said,

> *"A friend loves at all times and a brother is born for adversity." (Proverbs 17:17)*

Friendships should be like that. Friends should be with you in times of plenty and in times of want. No matter the situation, true friends are the ones who listen to you, cry with you, laugh with you, or give you a word of encouragement.

Prior to my job change, one friend quoted a Scripture verse to me several times. That verse was:

> *"The heart of man plans his way, but the Lord establishes his steps." (Proverbs 16:9)*

That verse resonates with me more after going through the valley with my job changing. God was directing my steps, and I needed to follow His way, not mine.

And now that verse hangs on my wall. It was a gift from another friend. Both friends have stayed close and encouraged me as I healed, processed God's new plan for me, and prayed for me as I wrote this book.

Solomon, the writer of Proverbs, tells us,

"A joyful heart is good medicine, but a crushed spirit dries up the bones." (Proverbs 17:22)

When my spirit was down these friends gave me joy. They encouraged me and increased my strength for the path that God had put me on. I didn't need to dwell in the valley, crushed by the weight of my circumstances, because their good medicine was based on the truths from God's Word. Their words had lifted my head up to praise Him and take joyful steps forward.

Key: Be encouraged and thankful for friends who support you.

Read: Proverbs 17:17; Proverbs 17:22

Action: What friends were like 'good medicine' and supported you during adversity? How can you support a friend who is struggling?

Prayer Moment: Lord, thank you for the friends who came alongside me. They have encouraged me and given me joy. Bless them today! Amen.

DAY THIRTY-SEVEN

Captive Thoughts

"Take every thought captive to obey Christ."
2 Corinthians 10:5

The first six months after my job change was tough. Tears and angry thoughts came often the first couple of weeks. The anger was like an annoying friend that would not go away. How could I get over this?

Have you been in a situation where you had similar feelings that were hard to let go? And you didn't know how you'd ever get back to a normal state that was void of those feelings.

I knew that I had to shake these feelings somehow and move on. It wasn't healthy for me to continue to be angry. I didn't want the anger to lead to resentment.

As these feelings came, I decided I would pray for God to take the thoughts captive to obedience to Christ. I would let them go and move on to the next thing.

"Take every thought captive to obey Christ." (2 Corinthians 10:5)

Then a memory or something said at a meeting at work would set off these thoughts all over again. That anger that I dealt with would resurface with triggers.

Triggers are words, sounds, pictures, or situations that bring a memory back from the past and put you back in that moment. Those who suffer from post-traumatic stress or have recovered from an addiction deal with triggers. But other hurtful situations can also be triggers.

Every time the thoughts came, I had to be diligent about taking them captive to Christ and immediately replace them with the truth of God's Word.

Paul told us to think about things that are true, honorable, just, pure, lovely, and commendable (Philippians. 4:8). I chose to think about Scripture that encouraged me.

God had removed me from a situation that was stressful and affecting my health. Satisfaction in my job had become my god, instead of Him.

There was one specific trigger that I remember clearly. I was at a manager meeting that I was having a hard time getting the courage up to attend. My former boss would be in this meeting, and it was hard to see him and not know what to say. And it was uncomfortable around other managers or leaders who didn't know what to say to me either.

I had decided to go anyway and paste a smile on my face. If there were times during the meeting when I felt angry or thought negative thoughts, I would quote this Scripture to myself,

> *"Forget what lies behind and strain forward to what lies ahead." (Philippians 3:13)*

God got me through this meeting, and He will do so in others like it. He helped me to leave the anger and other feelings behind me. He has a plan for me. That plan is to write a blog and book to help women find their contentment in God.

God has a plan for you and wants you to find your contentment in doing His plan. We may wonder and go off on many tangents to find that satisfaction on our own. But these paths won't satisfy, and anger or other destructive thoughts will befriend us.

We need to spend time in His presence and ask Him for help to remove these thoughts. He will direct us to His path that lies ahead.

Key: Take thoughts captive to reduce and eliminate frequent occurrences of anger, temptation, or other unholy thoughts.

Read: 2 Corinthians 10:5; Philippians 3:13-14; Philippians 4:8

Action: What is tripping you up? Anger, worry, fear, insecurity? Let go of it and ask God to take those thoughts captive. Do that *every* time the thoughts reoccur. Memorize a verse of God's truth that encourages you. When triggers come, rehearse that verse in your mind and let that thought go.

Prayer Moment: Lord, thank you for rescuing me from my situation. When triggers come, remind me of the Scripture that I need to combat this memory. Take that thought captive to the obedience of Christ. Replace the memory with Your truth. Amen.

DAY THIRTY-EIGHT

Walk With Integrity

*"May integrity and uprightness preserve me,
for I wait for you." Psalm 25:21*

When a person transfers jobs within a company, there are tasks from the old position to hand-off to the incoming manager. The new manager needs information, like vendor contacts, skills of the employees, the current projects, and financials for paying the bills.

I found myself in this position, having to hand-off responsibilities to a new manager. Even though my heart hurt from the sudden change of positions, I determined I would be respectful, kind, and honor Christ in every interaction with the new manager.

A couple of months later after the job transition, I ate lunch with the new manager of my former department. He said that I had been helpful to him in the transition and acted with integrity.

Have you been in an uncomfortable position of transferring knowledge or information to someone who was taking over your job or replacing you? Or maybe you said something that later you regretted?

Acting with integrity was a character trait that Paul wrote to Timothy about. He wanted each age group who were responsible for teaching others in the church to act in a specific way.

> *"Show yourself in all respects to be a model of good works, and in your teaching show integrity, dignity, and sound speech that cannot be condemned, so that an opponent may be put to shame, having nothing evil to say about us."* (Titus 2:7-8)

All groups were to be models of good works and teach with integrity so no one would say a bad thing about them.

They were to be a Christian witness to all people around them. If they didn't act with integrity, then the witness of their life would suffer. It would give others reason to gossip about how awful they were. And it would reflect poorly on Christ.

However, I recently said something that was not acting with integrity. I made a negative comment (yes, gossiping) to one of my coworkers about a person within our broader department. The next morning God convicted me of what I said, and I knew I needed to apologize to my co-worker. Once I was online, I told her that I needed to apologize. She started to dismiss what I had said.

I told her that I needed to apologize because as a Christian it reflected poorly on Christ and who I am. She accepted my apology and said I was forgiven.

When we are in a time of waiting on God, we need to act with integrity, respect, and sound speech. People are watching us to see how we act in these situations.

> *"May integrity and uprightness preserve me, for I wait for you." (Psalm 25:21)*

The Hebrew word for preserve in this verse is "*natsar*," which means to keep, observe, or guard with fidelity. Fidelity is defined as being faithful or loyal.

I love how David said that integrity and uprightness will preserve us as we wait. As we keep doing the right things that God has called us to do and act with integrity, we stay faithful and loyal to God. We know that He has a path for us, and we need to stick with it.

But His timing can be longer than what we expect. Even during a transition time, we need to act with integrity and righteousness while we wait for God's next step for us.

Key: Move forward with integrity and righteousness while you wait.

Read: Psalm 25:21; Titus 2:7-8

Action: How are your actions showing integrity? Can others tell that you are His? Do one thing today to identify with Christ and to show that you are a person of integrity.

Prayer Moment: Lord, help me to act with righteousness and integrity today. I need to be faithful and loyal to You in how I act as I wait for the next steps on my path. Amen.

DAY THIRTY-NINE

God Waits Too

"The Lord is not slow to fulfill his promise as some count slowness, but is patient toward you, not wishing that any should perish, but that all should reach repentance." 2 Peter 3:9

Waiting. It is so hard. Sometimes we wait years and even decades.

We keep an eye out for the perfect husband. We may anticipate the day that we will hold a baby in our arms, love them, and raise them to love God. Or maybe the waiting is for a house that we can call our own. Or maybe, we are waiting for that perfect job that we will enjoy doing.

Have you waited for something so long that you thought you'd never receive it?

A house is one thing I thought we would never receive. We lived in apartments and were tired of the inconveniences of it.

When our children were little, we found a duplex to rent. Living in a duplex was better, and we rarely heard noise through the shared wall with the neighbors.

The duplex was a good step in the right direction, but it still wasn't home. After living there for five years, we were able to put down a deposit on a house that we liked. We were finally home!

We had waited fourteen years for a house, but anything prior to that wasn't God's timing. Honestly, it would have been too hard for us financially. God wanted our obedience to His will. We had to wait for His perfect timing for our house.

Did you know that God waits too? He has been waiting since the beginning of time. When He created Adam and Eve, He had a personal relationship with them. But after the fall, when Adam and Eve sinned, man was separated from having close fellowship with God and He waits for us to repent and come to Him.

In the New Testament, Peter writes about Jesus returning someday and that He is slow in His coming. The Lord is waiting to return so all people, who are made in His image, will have a chance to repent, and come to Him. He doesn't want anyone to perish when the end of the world comes.

> *"The Lord is not slow to fulfill his promise as some count slowness, but is patient toward you, not wishing that any should perish, but that all should reach repentance." (2 Peter 3:9)*

Why do we wait so long to respond to Him? He is there waiting for us to repent or waiting for us to stop doing life on our own. Or maybe there is something that has become an idol that all our focus has been on it instead of God?

God is waiting for you. Will you come?

Key: Be aware that God waits on us too. Stop, pay attention, and listen to what He is saying. These steps are life-changing!

Read: Genesis 6:5; 2 Peter 3:9

Action: What one thing is God telling you lately that you need to stop and listen to Him? If He hasn't told you anything lately, what is one thing you can do to focus on Him more and listen to what God is saying to you?

Prayer Moment: Lord, thank you for Your patience with me! I come to You today and lay this one thing aside. I am listening to You. Help me to focus on what You want me to do. Amen.

Sanctifying Contact

"But you were washed, you were sanctified, you were justified in the name of the Lord Jesus Christ and by the Spirit of our God."
1 Corinthians 6:11

B eing in the presence of someone who is a celebrity, or a powerful figure can be exciting. Your heart races and trembles with excitement as you are around someone you admire.

Have you met someone of importance and trembled with excitement? Were you surprised and speechless? Or did you scream and talk with animation?

Moses had a similar experience, but his reaction was more extreme. He was leading his flock when he came to Mount Horeb, known as the mountain of God. And a bush was on fire but was not being destroyed by it. Moses was interested in the bush fire and drew near. Then God called to him:

> *"'Do not come near, take your sandals off your feet, for the place on which you are standing is holy ground.'" (Exodus 3:5)*

Moses did not tremble with excitement. He immediately took off his sandals and fell to the ground in fear.

Since God is holy, the ground was holy as well. The word for holy in Hebrew, "*qodesh*," means sacred or set apart. Moses was standing on holy ground and being sanctified as he communed with God.

He was calling Moses to do a special task. That task was to rescue the people from Egypt and take them to Israel, the Promised Land. God was sanctifying Moses for the task ahead.

God told the Israelites that He brought them out of Egypt to be their God, and they should "be holy as I am holy" (Leviticus 11:45).

In the New Testament, Paul wrote in his letter to the believers in Corinth,

> *"But you were washed, you were sanctified, you were justified in the name of the Lord Jesus Christ." (1 Corinthians 6:11)*

Sanctified means to be set apart, consecrated, or purified. Jesus washed away our sins, declared us righteous, and set us apart to serve God. And Jesus prayed for the disciples to do His holy work as well.

Before Jesus went to the cross, He prayed for the disciples. He prayed they'd be sanctified in the truth of the words of God. Jesus consecrated Himself to do holy work so that the disciples could be sanctified in truth (John 17:17, 19).

Being in contact with God, Jesus, and the Holy Spirit through the truths in His Word purifies us. This connection with God's Word daily infuses us with His presence. And whenever we meet Him, we are standing on holy ground.

We need to be in God's Word daily as we wait on Him. This time with Him and His Word sanctifies us to be holy as He is holy. Like God preparing Moses, His Word is preparing us for the work that He has called us to do.

Be encouraged as you wait. Enjoy the sanctifying contact with God as He molds and shapes you into the person you need to be, so you are ready for the task ahead.

Key: Constant contact with God continues the sanctifying process.

Read: Leviticus 11:45; John 17:17, 19; 1 Corinthians 6:11

Action: What are you doing to protect your sanctifying contact time with God? Make a specific appointment time with God and protect that sacred time with Him.

Prayer Moment: Lord, I thank you that You sanctified me through Jesus. And I can become holy by spending time with You. I will wait and enjoy this time with You while you prepare me for the task You have ahead for me. Amen.

Strength Training

"God, the Lord, is my strength;
He makes my feet like the deer's;
He makes me tread on my high places."
Habakkuk 3:19

Have you been in a situation where the circumstances seemed impossible to manage? Were you anxious? What did you do to handle this daunting task?

As I walked into the building after being humiliated by the sudden change in my job, the task ahead seemed impossible. I had wanted to run and hide by going to a different job but that was not what God wanted me to do. I had already agreed to stay and learn from this situation in this place and time.

As I thought through my situation, I reminded myself of His love for me and that He was giving me strength even though I felt so weak. And then the hymn, *Jesus Loves Me*, came to my mind. The first verse of that song is:

"Jesus loves me, this I know, for the Bible tells me so. Little ones to Him belong, they are weak, but he is strong." (William Batchelder Bradbury)

The last few words struck me. When I am weak, He is strong. He gives me the strength to go on. I could get through this day with His strength, not mine.

The Old Testament prophet, Habakkuk, closed out his prophetic book with a prayer that echoes this same sentiment. He was praying that even though there weren't blossoms on the fig trees or fruit on the vines, the crops weren't yielding any food, and there weren't cattle in the stalls, He could rejoice in God, His salvation (Habakkuk 3:17-18).

Even though the circumstances were dire, Habakkuk concluded,

"God, the Lord, is my strength; He makes my feet like the deer's; He makes me tread on my high places." (Habakkuk 3:19)

God Himself was giving him the strength to get through this trial or, like the deer, to walk on high places.

I am amazed how deer and other similar animals can walk among rocks on mountains without an easy way to hang on. Yet the deer have the agility to jump from rock to rock and cling to the rocks with their hooves. They don't seem to be afraid of the high mountains either.

God's strength had given Habakkuk's feet the ability to stand where he normally could not do it on his own. His high place was living in a land that was devastated. Yet, he was moving forward with the feet that enabled him to do the impossible. He was believing God would provide for him and give him the strength to continue.

My high place was walking into work and into the new position. I was afraid of what others would say about me. A simple song about Jesus loving me and strengthening me empowered me to move forward into the day.

When I lean on myself, I fail to move forward due to my weakness. However, the more I lean on Jesus, I am strengthened by His presence. It is strength training for my spirit.

Like a spotter in weightlifting who pushes the weightlifter to lift more weight, God is asking us to do more in life. However, God doesn't ask us or push us to do it alone. He gives us the strength to do the unthinkable and walks alongside us.

What is your high place? Where is it that you need God's strength to stand? Is it a high mountain top, a devastated wasteland, or a weak moment where you need God's strength to get through it?

Hold onto your belief that God's strength will get you through hard situations. You are doing strength training with God to prepare for those times when the task seems impossible.

Key: Lean on God's strength even when you are weak. This enables you to stand or remain standing in impossible places.

Read: Habakkuk 3:17-19

Action: Name one thing you can do today to rely on God's strength while you wait.

Prayer Moment: God, my Lord, You are my strength. Thank you for giving me the strength I need to get through tough times. You enable me to stand. Keep training me to lean on You so I will be ready to stand when the task seems impossible. Amen.

New Things Ahead

"'Behold, I am doing a new thing; now it springs forth. Do you not perceive it?'" Isaiah 43:19

The roads were dusty. Then after the rain, they were a muddy mess. Every day, ten minutes to 7 a.m., the construction equipment rumbled down the road before they began digging. Periodically, I closed the windows to muffle the sound so I could work in silence.

Even with the mess and loud sounds, our neighborhood was buzzing from the excitement. The neighbor's kids watched nearby as the large excavator dug out mounds of dirt. When my husband arrived home from work, he'd rush outside to video the happenings to share them with our grandsons who love construction equipment.

Have you lived in a construction zone or driven your car through one? Does your life feel like a muddy mess at times?

Isaiah, an Old Testament prophet, was told by the Lord the people would experience hard times. There would be times where they'd feel like they were going through the fire, but God would not allow them to be consumed by it. Or times where the trials would be like floods, but they would not be overtaken by them (Isaiah 43:2).

They did not need to fear because God was working among them. He was providing ways for them to be brought back to Israel. Yet people were not believing in what God could do and was doing. He reminded them that He was the Lord and no other one would save them (Isaiah 43:11).

He told them to forget the former things of the past. He said,

> *"'Behold, I am doing a new thing; now it springs forth. Do you not perceive it?'" (Isaiah 43:19)*

God was doing something new, like spring flowers popping up through the previously dormant soil. He would make a pathway in the wilderness and even a river in a desert. Once they were on the other side, they could praise God for making a way forward.

Dry and arid land with refreshing water to drink seems like an oxymoron. But God does this and more with His amazing power.

When there seems to be a rough landscape that I am encountering, God is doing something new with my life and I need to rely on God's strength to empower me to get me through it to the other side. As He is bringing me through the trials, He is molding me and shaping me for new things ahead. When I praise Him for all He has brought me through and done in my life, I can wait in expectation for what is to come.

Forget the painful memories of the past. Look beyond the messy roads of construction that are around you and see the things that God has done for you. Hang on tight as the water rises or the fire comes close. God will guide you through it and be with you.

He is doing something new in your life. Build up the excitement for it as you wait. And once you arrive on the freshly paved roads, belt out a big, "Praise the Lord"!

Key: Even though there are roads ahead under construction, God is doing a new thing. Wait with expectation.

Read: Isaiah 43:2-19; 2 Corinthians 6:3-10

Action: What are you waiting on God for with expectation? Claim the promise that He is doing a new thing. You may not see it yet but wait with hopeful expectation.

Prayer Moment: Lord, thank you for getting me through the messy construction in my life. Thank you for the new things ahead. I wait in expectation for what You will do. Amen.

DAY FORTY-THREE

God's Plan for Purpose

"Many are the plans in the mind of a man, but it is the purpose of the Lord that will stand."
Proverbs 19:21

I had big plans of being promoted at work and becoming a director. These were the plans that were in my mind, and I thought they were the best plan for me.

Since education has been a love of mine since I was young, I went to graduate school to learn how to be a better manager within Information Technology.

When I graduated, instead of the promotion I hoped for, there was a new boss at work. Eventually, I found myself choosing between a layoff or a position in another department.

Did you have great plans for yourself that fell through? What was it? Did you feel disheartened and angry like I did?

I realized that God must have a better plan than the one that I had for me. After all, God's purposes are proven to be the best for us.

> *"Many are the plans in the mind of man, but it is the purpose of the Lord that will stand." (Proverbs 19:21)*

Once I was released from my plan, I asked God what purpose He had for me. I thought about my desire for writing a book that I had shelved years earlier. Could this be God's plan for me?

God uses His Word and other believers to tell us about His plans for us. Solomon, the writer of Proverbs, said,

> *"The fear of the Lord is the beginning of wisdom, and knowledge of the Holy One is insight" (Proverbs 9:10)*

When I spend time in God's Word, I learn more about Him. And the more I know of Him, the more I am in awe of who He is. This is what is meant by the fear of the Lord in this verse. Reverential fear of the Lord births wisdom in us. We become insightful about how to do this life and what is the most important to God becomes valuable as well.

The psalmist says that we are blessed when we walk in the light of the Lord's Face (Psalm 89:15). When I look to God for His purpose for me and spend time with Him daily, I am blessed. Not only by being in His presence but by walking the path that He wants me to be on. And that path is to share with women how they can find contentment in His plan.

Nothing else we desire in this life will satisfy us. Not a promotion at work, not a husband, not children, not a house, not extravagant things, or any other thing that we are putting in place of God. None of these things will bring us the fulfillment that we long for.

Spend time reading God's Word, seeking His Face in prayer, and seek out the plans for the purpose He has in your life. His plans are far better than anything we can look for on our own. He will give you a plan that will be accomplished, and you will find contentment in Him.

Key: Listening and communing with God allows you to hear and accomplish the purpose He has for you.

Read: Psalm 89:15; Proverbs 9:10; Proverbs 19:21

Action: What is one talent you have that you can use for God? How can you use that talent for Him today?

Prayer Moment: Lord, thank you for the talents that You have given me. How should I use them today? Lead me to the plan that You have for me to do. Amen.

Run With Endurance

"Let's rid ourselves of every obstacle and the sin which so easily entangles us, and let's run with endurance the race that is set before us." Hebrews 12:1

The day was hot with the temperature in the 90's and high humidity. The heat was rising from the blacktop. Sweat was dripping down my forehead from beneath my helmet. And I was running out of water. How can I continue this long bike ride, I asked myself?

For several years, my husband and I have been involved in a bike fundraiser from the Twin Cities to our Bible camp in Northeast Iowa. It is a one-way bike ride of 185 miles of rolling hills on two-lane highways over the course of three days.

With any bike trip of this nature, there are obstacles to overcome—extreme heat, rainy days, high winds which push you back, road construction, gravel, roadkill, and even bike accidents. With prayer and physical endurance, we were able to bike around these hurdles and get to the finish line. By doing this, we have raised thousands of dollars for special projects for campers to enjoy while at camp.

Have you experienced similar barriers in exercise or life and wanted to quit?

In my life, I have experienced obstacles that tried to keep me from running the race God has for me. There have been layoffs, financial worries, desires for promotion, anxiety, stress, and health issues. Most of these hurdles have resulted from my own choices and were keeping me from doing God's plan. I chose to go another way or took my eyes off God and what He had for me. If I had stayed with God's plan for my life, the unnecessary suffering of anxiety and stress would have been avoidable.

The writer of Hebrews said,

> *"Let's rid ourselves of every obstacle and the sin which so easily entangles us, and let's run with endurance the race that is set before us." (Hebrews 12:1)*

As the Greek defines the word, *euperistatos*, for entangle, these burdens are skillfully surrounding us. Sin has a way of doing that. Once we take one step in its direction and get a taste of what appears to bring us pleasure, we are enclosed by it, and it is hard to find a way out.

Once we throw those entangling sins aside, however, we can run ahead with endurance in whatever race we are in. We may want to quit because of these hurdles. However, we can persevere because we have the example of Christ to follow. We are to **look**

> *"to Jesus, the founder and perfecter of our faith, who for the joy that was set before him endured the cross, despising the shame, and is seated at the right hand of the throne of God." (Hebrews 12:2)*

We need to look to Jesus as we encounter these trials. The Greek word for look, *aphorao*, means to turn our eyes away from something else and keep our eyes fixed on Him. Jesus endured the cross and reached the finish line by sitting down next to God in heaven. Since He persevered through the shame and all that pain on our behalf, He is the model of endurance to help us finish our race.

Discard anything that is keeping you from the path that God has for you and your contentment. Keep your eyes fixed on Jesus who is there at the finish line waiting for you to cross. He is the One to follow and keep you determined to make it to the end of your course.

Key: Throw off the entangling sin and run with determined perseverance to finish the race.

Read: Hebrews 12:1-2

Action: What is one thing you can do today to maintain the determination to finish your current race?

Prayer Moment: Lord, I throw off these encompassing sins and give them to You. I look to Jesus for help. Give me the endurance to finish my race. Amen.

AUTHOR'S NOTE

Dear Friend,

Since you have journeyed with me on how God used the change in my position to grow closer to Him and being content in His plan, I wanted to share the next adventure in that plan.

Before sending my edited copy of this book to publishers, I got a new job! With each interview, I asked God to open the doors if this is where He wanted me to be or close the doors and put up glaring red flags. Throughout the process, it became clear that God wanted me at this new company and the doors and windows flew open! They gave me an offer for the position, I accepted. And I have now been employed there for one year.

It is amazing to see how God has worked out his immeasurable and unimaginable plan in my life!

He can do this in your life too! Keep letting go of your self-made plans so you can be content in His plan and rejoice in your work.

Praying you find contentment in His plan,
Cindy

APPENDIX

Peace with God

You can know God and **Know Peace**! If you haven't asked Jesus Christ to be your Lord and Savior, God wants a relationship with you!

God loves you and He desires to have a close relationship with you. We all were designed from the beginning to have relationships. God wants one with you too! When we have a close relationship with Him, we can **know peace**.

That is why His inspired and inerrant Word says in:

2 Peter 3:9 (ESV) The Lord is not slow to fulfill his promise as some count slowness, but is patient toward you, not wishing that any should perish, but that all should reach repentance.

He wants everyone in the world to have a relationship with Him! He loves all of us and sent His Son, Jesus Christ, to die an awful death on the cross. The difference between Jesus dying and any other prophet is that He rose again from the dead. Then He appeared to many people within 40 days after His resurrection. He even appeared to 500 people at one time! (See 1 Corinthians 15:3-6)

We need to respond to Him today. By doing so, we have **PEACE** in this life and then have eternal life with Him when we die. We will have struggles in this world. But God is with us as He said, "I will never leave you nor forsake you" (Hebrews 13:5).

You can know peace with God by reading these verses and take the steps outlined on this website: Steps to Peace.org.

If you accept Jesus Christ as your Lord and Savior as you read God's Word and this devotional, please email me at: cindy@godsplanguidedsteps.com and let me know. I would love to celebrate that with you!

READ Study Method

The READ study method is based on the several years that I have facilitated inductive Bible studies for women. The steps are as follows:

1. **R**eady yourself in prayer - Pray before you study. Ask God to quiet your mind and take captive thoughts and distractions (2 Corinthians 10:5). Invite the Holy Spirit to guide you and give you the insight into God's Word.

2. **E**xamine the scriptures – Write down the verses. Look at the context, or the verses around it, that help you understand what it means. Write down key words. These are words that have a distinct meaning that helps you interpret Scripture. Read the verse in different Bible translations. Write down the key words that stand out in the other

versions. Next, pretend you are a journalist. Answer questions of who, what, why, when, where, and how. Write down notes about concepts learned, promises given or fulfilled, and significant things that are meaningful to you

3. **A**pplication – write down what this means to you and what you can apply to your life from this study.
4. **D**eclare – Write a prayer of declaration to God about learnings and how you can apply it to your life. If you need help, ask Him to help you achieve it.

Note: A Hebrew Greek Key Word Study Bible is very useful. If you don't have one, you can to these helpful free resources: BlueLetterBible.com website or download the application for Blue Letter Bible on your phone.

These READ study method instructions, sample study and a sheet to print out for your study notes can be found in the Resource Library on my website: GodsPlanGuidedSteps.com.

Notes

1. Barb Peil, *www://barbpeil.com.*

Acknowledgments

To God be the glory! If God had not gotten my attention with my job change, this book would not have come to fruition. Thank you, Lord, Jesus, and Holy Spirit, for redirecting, guiding, and leading me to the plan that You have for me. It has brought me great peace and joy to be working within Your Will!

To my husband, Dave, who spent time alone or hours playing with our dog without me. He has been supportive in this endeavor, and I couldn't have done this without his love, encouragement, and true friendship. Love you, honey!

To my prayer team, Ginny, JoAnn, and Amie – you have been the undergirding strength behind this work. I don't know how this book would have become a reality without all the prayers that you brought before God's throne! You are all amazing prayer warriors!

To friends who asked along the way how it was going and encouraged me to continue, I appreciate you more than you know. God brought your words to motivate me and spur me on. Thank you, Jo, and others, you know who you are.

To my editor, Melanie Chitwood. I appreciate your expertise and words of wisdom. It was an honor and a privilege to be under your tutelage. Thank you!

To my dear friend, Jen, who did a friend edit of a few devotions. Your eye for catching the details after a couple hours of reading was the set of eyes needed to help me finish the work and rejoice that it was done. I am so thankful for you, your God-given gifts, and most of all your friendship!

CINDY SCHWERDTFEGER

About the Author

Cindy Schwerdtfeger is a writer, wife to Dave, mom to two Jesus-loving grown children and their spouses, four spunky grandkids, and one rambunctious black lab mix. For over thirty-six years, Cindy has taught God's Word to children, youth, and women in her local church in the Twin Cities, MN. For the past nineteen years, she has focused on teaching women through inductive Bible studies. You can read more about how you can find contentment in God's plan on her website: GodsPlanGuidedSteps.com.

Made in USA - Kendallville, IN
35292_9798218074241
10.14.2022 1304